LOVE ONLINE

A Practical Guide to Digital Dating

Phyllis Phlegar

▲▼ Addison-Wesley Publishing Company
Reading, Massachusetts   Menlo Park, California   New York
Don Mills, Ontario   Wokingham, England   Amsterdam   Bonn
Sydney   Singapore   Tokyo   Madrid   San Juan
Paris   Seoul   Milan   Mexico City   Taipei

Many of the designations used by manufacturers and sellers to distinguish their products are claimed as trademarks. Where those designations appear in this book, and Addison-Wesley was aware of a trademark claim, the designations have been printed in initial capital letters or all capital letters.

The authors and publishers have taken care in preparation of this book, but make no expressed or implied warranty of any kind and assume no responsibility for errors or omissions. No liability is assumed for incidental or consequential damages in connection with or arising out of the use of the information or programs contained herein.

Library of Congress Cataloging-in-Publication Data

Phlegar, Phyllis.
  Love online : a practical guide to digital dating / Phyllis Phlegar.
       p.   cm.
  ISBN 0-201-40965-8
  1. Computer bulletin boards.   2. Dating (Social customs)
3. Interpersonal communication.   I. Title.
QA76.9.B84P46   1995
025.06'30673--dc20   94-44019
                                                                  CIP

Copyright © 1995 by Phyllis Phlegar

Boardwatch Magazine articles © March 1994. Reprinted with permission from *Boardwatch Magazine* and publisher Jack Rickard.

All rights reserved. No part of this publication may be reproduced, stored in a retrieval system, or transmitted, in any form or by any means, electronic, mechanical, photocopying, recording, or otherwise, without the prior written permission of the publisher. Printed in the United States of America. Published simultaneously in Canada.

Sponsoring Editor: Claire Horne
Project Manager: Eleanor McCarthy
Production Coordinator: Lora L. Ryan
Cover design: Jean Seal
Cover Illustration: Dan Sneberger
Text design: Karen Battles
Set in 11.5 point Berkeley Oldstyle by Battles Design

1 2 3 4 5 6 7 8 9 - DOH - 9998979695
First printing, January 1995

Addison-Wesley books are available for bulk purchases by corporations, institutions, and other organizations. For more information please contact the Corporate, Government, and Special Sales Department at (800) 238-9682.

*To Hal, my husband,
who deserves only good things.*

CONTENTS

CHAPTER ONE
Love Online: What Is It? ▶ 1

CHAPTER TWO
What You Need to Know Before Going Online ▶ 21

CHAPTER THREE
Hot Chats and Hot Tubs: Advice for the Interested ▶ 45

CHAPTER FOUR
Bulletin Boards ▶ 69

CHAPTER FIVE
The Commercial Online Services ▶ 111

CHAPTER SIX
The Internet ▶ 147

APPENDIX ▶ 171

GLOSSARY ▶ 177

Acknowledgments

Without Ken Totura, I would not have written this book. I met Ken in the spring of '91, right after I was hired at CW Electronics in Denver. At the time I was not online anywhere and I was using a borrowed XT computer that didn't even have a modem. Ken told me to buy a modem and gave me the software containing the Prodigy ID that I still use today. I'd also like to thank Sandy and the other employees at CW, and Patrick and Mike from Software Etc., for dealing kindly with me when I knew practically nothing about computing.

Many thanks to Thom Foulks for putting me together with *Boardwatch Magazine*. Next in the chain of events—thanks to my editors at *Boardwatch*, Brian Gallagher and Jack Rickard, who published the articles that caught the attention of Claire Horne of Addison-Wesley, who bravely asked if I'd write this book.

Several folks were particularly instrumental in holding my hand while I was writing, including Harold Day, Michael Knapp, my parents, Leon and Estelle Kopelman, and my sister, Fran Aufrect. Also thanks to my old friend Dan Kilby, a certified hypnotherapist, longtime BBSer, and traveler on several national services. Dan spent hours with me, sharing his insights on the psychology of the cyberspace community.

A special thanks to the sysops and the gang from The Male Box, to Dave Cunningham of CompuServe, Shannon Wilson and Peter Helmer of Prodigy, Pam McGraw of America Online, the gang from Collectibles on GEnie, Kristine Loosley of BBS Direct/CRIS, and author and longtime Delphi member, Ted Remington. And thank you to those who made various helpful contributions, including John Morris, Jason Salas, Ed Hoffman, Harvey Heagy, Kelly Bradley, Jan Redding, Deborah Robbins, Joyce Neighbors, and to my former fifth-grade teacher, Joyce Dalton. Many thanks for all the insight and information from the folks who would prefer to remain anonymous, but whose information helped shape this effort. I also want to acknowledge my flight instructor, James Douglas Lane, for daring me to keep learning—at any age.

CHAPTER ONE

▶

Love Online: What Is It?

Love online. It sounds intriguing, but what is it? Love is many different things to many people, but generally speaking, love involves strong, positive feelings toward someone else. What's "online"? Being online means using a computer and a modem (a device that acts as an interface between your computer and a telephone line) to communicate with other people using computers and modems—so you're all hooked up together via the phone lines. While you're online you can search through vast archives of information; you can tap into a wealth of discussions and experiences from every corner of the globe, or from just down the street. I think of it as being in touch with many minds without the bother of having to go anywhere physically.

Ever try to get your neighbor on the phone and you keep getting a busy signal? Finally he or she answers and says something like, "Sorry, I was online." What *were* they doing online for hours? "Oh, I was talking to this person in Maine, and we were discussing whether the lobster really should be on the state license tag," or "I was cruising the adult area to see if my Friday night computer date was online," or "I was reading my email and replying to a few people."

What has happened, unnoticed by many people, is that a growing number of people have found communicating through a computer to be a big part of their lives. Through the Internet, the commercial services like **Prodigy** or **America Online**, and **bulletin board systems** (BBSs), the number of people with computer connections has grown at such a rate that if someone isn't actually online already, they've heard about being online from friends, newspapers and magazines, or TV and radio.

You can argue that computers freeze people in a state of isolation, in which they stare at a computer screen for hours at a time without physical human contact. The reverse of that argument is that going online provides opportunities for people to socialize, exchange ideas, meet others, and make friends more easily than it might be for them to do so offline. The number of people you can talk to in one day on your computer is staggering; in many senses, it's the antithesis of isolation!

After all, one thing that human beings like to do is talk. We've always talked—around the campfire, over the backyard fence, in the supermarket, in cafés and coffee shops—and now we're talking, chatting, debating, ranting, raving, loving, and even having sex through a computer and a modem. And all this talking can take place via local, national, or international venues.

So we could say that love online is loving someone platonically, emotionally, or even sexually, based on what can be known about them after many conversations on the computer. It may sound like an odd way to fall in love, but it's happening and has been since people with modems found each other and started talking via their keyboards.

LOVE ON THE WIRES

Strictly speaking, a sexual affair or romance requires that both parties be in real physical contact at some point. But romance in the online universe (known as **cyberspace**) requires little more than a computer, a modem, and an ability to make conversation. And human nature being what it is, sometimes the conversations in cyberspace tend toward the erotic. (The slang words for computer-mediated erotic activity are computer sex, **cybersex**, or **c-sex**.)

Mention computer sex to computer illiterates, and they may well turn up their noses and look disgusted. That's an understandable reaction if you don't know what this world of online communication is all about and don't consider the mind's limitless possibilities combined with the lure of the written word. Cybersex can be as crude as "talking dirty" via **email** (electronic mail sent between two people online) or the activity can occur on a more elevated level of thoughtful prose and exotic erotica. Typically what happens is that, by design or accident, two people meet someplace online and become attracted to each other through common interests, or they simply become drawn to the personality flowing through the wires and onto the computer screen. Carefully at first, they begin to ask personal questions. They may begin to meet online, as couples in the "real" world do, more and more frequently. Eventually, via the typed words they exchange, their relationship becomes more intimate, and the people involved may begin to feel emotionally dependent in a way that feels like, and is, love.

Cybersex can be, and often is, very compelling. Making love and finding love online is something you have to do yourself in order to understand it fully. There is no direct comparison in the physical world; mail and the phone are distant cousins to computer communication. A computer and a modem can make all the difference in a long-distance relationship because you don't have to wait for a letter through the mail (and for the most part, the news you'd read is old news by the time you get it) or go broke calling on the phone constantly. People tend to be very open and relaxed online; they often feel free to be themselves in ways they might not in person. The open and almost instantaneous mental connection can make a romance by email surprisingly satisfying, although markedly different from the traditional love affair.

A WARNING ABOUT ILLICIT ONLINE ROMANCE

People in committed, real-life relationships often go to the computer world of romance for recreational "sex"; sometimes they are looking to fill the gaps in an unfulfilling or dying relationship. And while meeting people and playing around online seems as harmless as a racy book or erotic movie, sometimes online flirtations end up going a lot farther than the parties intended and get complicated without warning. You're dealing with real people, even though they may have manufactured identities, and those people may expect something from you (a commitment, a permanent connection, or more emotional connection than you feel) despite having never seen you nor heard your voice. Also, the developing "affair" is easily hidden from others. The ease with which people can communicate without being noticed by others (partners and spouses included) allows relationships to develop quickly and perhaps more easily than might happen otherwise.

It doesn't take a lot of online time before it is difficult to think of your friends "in the computer" as anything but real and capable of having a noticeable effect on your life. There are many people who have spent a long time looking for a life mate without success—many have found the bar scene or blind dates poor vehicles for meeting compatible, interesting people. The computer may be just the place for that type of person to meet people from all over the world and to have a chance to get to know them well before anything occurs physically. Friendships blossom effortlessly, and some of them can and do last a lifetime. Common interest groups often have yearly get-togethers where they can see each other face to face, hear each other's voices, and then go back online after it's over and have a face and a voice to go with the name on the screen.

SO, HOW DO PEOPLE ACTUALLY COMMUNICATE ON THE COMPUTER?

Think of the process of making a phone call. The connection is similar in some ways, but instead of picking up the phone and dialing, your **modem** (a device that connects your computer to the telephone line), on command from your computer, dials a number you've typed in. Let's say you're dialing a bulletin board system (more on the different types of those later). When the number you've dialed answers (via its modem), the two modems "shake hands" (communication flows between them in a controlled manner). If all goes well, you're "logged onto" the online world. The service or BBS will probably ask you a few simple questions to get you registered. For some of the large, national services, special software will work with your modem to get you online. Each bulletin board or service is a little different, but basically they all use the phone lines to connect. Local BBSs and most of the national services have either a toll-free number or a **local node** (a point that you dial into to connect to the system) for you to use, which eliminates long-distance charges. You can literally be wired to exchange words globally.

You'll find that managing your time is easier online than in the rest of your life, especially if you're very busy. The bulletin boards and email boxes are open twenty-four hours a day. Since there's no dress code, you can communicate from the comfort of your home, hotel room, or office—literally anywhere there is a phone line and a computer with a modem.

You'll also discover an ease of expression that might not exist in the rest of your life. (If you're a pretty good typist, that is.) People have come up with a wide variety of creative methods for communicating facial expressions, tone of voice, body language, and so on via the keyboard. See Chapter Four for conventions regarding typing and communicating online.

WHO'S ONLINE AND WHAT ARE THEY DOING?

People are online for a wide variety of reasons: to prosper professionally; to seek information; to make business contacts; to pursue hobbies and special interests; to meet people and communicate with them—about anything and everything—and, frankly, there are those people that go online to "talk dirty" or offensively to other people. While some people fall exclusively into one category or another, most online citizens are there for a combination of these reasons. People of all colors, shapes, and sizes are online, either to find others like themselves or, just as frequently, people who are not like them. In the online world, we can leave aside issues of body or gender because, after all, that's what the online world offers us: the ability to be what we "look like mentally" as opposed to what we look like physically.

Communicating via computer seems to be an excellent medium for people who feel uneasy in any way about their attractiveness—they are freed from the constraints of a society that judges people so often on physical characteristics. Only a person's personality comes across on a computer, and it is the first chance many people have had to communicate free of the trappings of their body.

For a long time, there were many more men than women online. Men dominated the computer industry for a long time and still pretty much do. Though there still are more men than women online, the gap is narrowing quickly. Not only are more women entering the field of computers and online communications in general, but more members of the general population are buying modem-equipped computers and logging onto the

Internet, BBSs, and commercial services just to see what this information superhighway hype is all about.

The gay and lesbian community is online in force, with their own local bulletin boards and common interest areas on the national services. The restraints of society are no doubt the reason why many gay people are online. Whatever your opinion might be of people with alternative lifestyles and sexual preferences, it's a fact that being "different" can make people reticent to open up and be themselves. But online—at least in certain places—this type of revelation seems safer and easier. For someone with an alternative lifestyle, particularly someone who lives in a conservative part of the country, the freedom of the online world provides a relaxed avenue of expression.

Folks with special physical needs can "run faster" online than they can otherwise. For example, someone in a wheelchair might experience this type of communicating, talking, and traveling through cyberspace as wonderfully liberating. Access to an online forum gives someone who is disabled or otherwise isolated due to location or lifestyle terrific freedom to move about and socialize on a scale that was not possible before. If you're living in a secluded place—or in an unfamiliar country—online communications can be a real lifesaver. The computer watering hole is always open, full of interesting people who are glad to see you come around and join the party.

College and high-school students are a formidable presence online, and as home computers proliferate, even younger, elementary-age children, often alone and unsupervised, can be found among the cybercommunity. Obviously this brings special kinds of problems. A computer may seem like a harmless toy, but imagine the ramifications of a child getting online and into an adult area. Unscrupulous people inhabit cyberspace too; much that could hurt a child exists online. You should always be aware of kids online, pretending to be adults. Teenagers are especially likely to do this—but it's usually fairly easy to call their bluff with a few key questions (see Chapter Two, Kids Online).

Making friends with the varied group of people in the online world is an opportunity you might not get otherwise because of society's prejudices, and perhaps some of your own of which you were unaware. When you meet someone online and get to like them, preconceptions or biases about their looks, and yours, suddenly seem much less important.

DECEPTION

As you might have expected, there's a downside to not being able to see who you're talking to. Some people can, and do, pass themselves off as something they are not, be it younger, older, prettier, thinner, or even a different sex. Some folks take on a false identity in order to see what it feels like to "be" someone else. And though masquerading as someone else can be very interesting and a unique opportunity to learn a few things, if you do so for any length of time, it's really not fair to people who may think they are getting to know—not to mention like—the "real" you.

The online world has its other similarities to life off line. Unfortunately, the dishonest live, and often thrive, in cyberspace. Some people are con artists trying to extort money or something else of value from people online. Others will woo you over the computer in an attempt to meet you **IRL** (in Real Life) for some **s2s** (skin to skin) with as little compassion or concern as the person looking for a one-night stand in a bar. (If some of the abbreviations, like s2s, sound silly to you, I agree; but they do describe the activity quickly and accurately, and many onliners use them often.) Other people are pathologically lonely, depressed, or co-dependent individuals who probably need professional help. Every flavor of person is represented online, and you should keep that in mind as you explore the airwaves.

Further, people tend to invest themselves, to different degrees, in their online relationships. Though they're just reading text on a computer screen, real emotions and expectations get built up through online encounters. Cyberspace may seem like an unreal place, since no one has a physical presence online; but if you get hurt, which you may, it will feel very much the same as it does IRL. If and when you get involved, be cautious; learn how to avoid the bad situations at the same time that you learn to recognize the good ones.

For example, there was no way for me to know when I logged on for the first time in June 1991 that I would meet my future husband in less than thirty days, as well as a good friend who lives just a few miles away, and other friends in other cities and towns to whom I still talk online. Though I was the greenest of novices, I have a natural tendency toward caution, and I think it kept me out of trouble. Maybe it's because I wasn't looking for anyone or anything in particular and did a lot of **surfing** (also called **cruising** or **skimming**), and lots of reading and waiting. You might consider adopting the same attitude as you start out in the online world.

The technology does exist for people to attach a special camera to their computer, which can send and receive pictures online (if the person you're communicating with has the same type of equipment). Frankly, no matter how affordable and available the video technology becomes, using it right away defeats the purpose of getting to know someone's mind without the distraction of a visual dimension. There will come a time when pictures are exchanged, but there is nothing like meeting face-to-face, or f2f, the very first time.

TALK CAN BE CHEAP

It's expected that soon every computer sold will be equipped with a modem. And the price of *everything* online has dropped and should continue to drop, from commercial services to dozens of Internet access providers offering cheap or even free communications software. You can buy a computer that can get you online for only a few hundred dollars; it won't be anywhere near state of the art, but it will serve the purpose. And your ride on the cybertrain of a national service can cost less than $10 a month. Years ago, that was close to the hourly rate. For less than $200, you can find an obsolete (but still useful) IBM-compatible laptop with a modem that goes online everywhere on most of the services that don't require Windows; it's great on trips if you want to stay in touch with cyberfriends while you are away. You don't have to be rich to be online. Even a "fully dressed" computer can be had for less than two grand, including a spiffy, speedy modem.

Let's Talk Terms

The popularity of PCs and modems in the home and workplace has led to bulletin boards sprouting and commercial services and the Internet growing at an amazing pace. While you've probably heard about a certain information superhighway, it's a safe bet that a lot of people still don't know what it is and what the associated technical terms and buzzwords mean. Here are a few of the important terms:

The **Internet**, also known as "The Net," is a connected network of online communities linking the worlds of education, government, business, and individuals all over the world. The Internet began as a U.S. government-funded network used by the military and various defense-related agencies in order to exchange information and share hardware and software resources.

Bulletin board Systems (commonly abbreviated as BBSs) are a lot like actual bulletin boards, only instead of the familiar structure that hangs on a wall, these "boards" exist online. Each board has its own phone number, which people dial into for connection. On the board you'll find various messages, or **postings**, related to the board's specific subject area or interest. You'll discover lengthy and in-depth conversational histories out there in cyberspace.

The commercial information services such as **CompuServe, Prodigy, America Online, Delphi, GEnie**, and **BBS Direct/CRIS** offer an incredible array of online services for a set monthly fee. In some cases you log on to these services using their own software; then you can explore the special-interest forums and exhaustive databases, exchange email and download files, and even access the Internet (in a more or less restricted form). For more information on commercial services, see Chapter Five.

Email is, literally, electronic mail. When someone sends you email, it is a private "mailing" that waits for you in your **electronic mailbox** (emailbox) until you elect to review it. Everyone likes getting email. All the national services and most BBSs send a piece of welcome mail to you immediately after logging on so that you feel part of the action right away. Some of the local, privately owned and operated BBSs have email that is considered private, but the **sysop** (**sys**tem **op**erator, the knowledgeable person overseeing board activity) can, and sometimes does, read it. Some states hold the sysop responsible in some part if illegal or illicit activity is occurring on his or her board. So, sometimes a sysop reads email, but no one else will see it. On the Internet and most of the commercial services, email is not read by anyone except the person it was intended for; any other treatment borders on illegal.

Flames are angry postings or exchanges of hostile or ill-tempered email. Don't be surprised if you encounter plenty of this online. Because it's so easy to type what's on your mind, extremes of personality are sometimes all too evident. People love to vent, rage, and let off steam online. If you spend any amount of time online, expect to be flamed by someone at some point.

I know it's hard to imagine what going online is like if you've never done it. Take a look at Figures 1-1 and 1-2; these show welcome screens that you'll see when **signing on** (making the initial connection to a specific online site) to a bulletin board and to the America Online commercial service. Some services and many BBSs are text-based, which means that you see only words and menus composed of words on your screen or monitor when on the service or BBS. Then there are services such as America Online that are based on a graphical user interface (**GUI**); you point your mouse and click on icons and pictures to navigate through the service. Some BBSs have started offering a graphical user interface, but many are still text-based. To sign on to a BBS, you use a communications program that tells your modem what number to dial. When the BBS or national service answers on the other end of the line, either you or the program tells them who's calling and where you want to go.

Prodigy and America Online (AOL) have their own software that you are required to use when signing on. Once you've followed all the directions and managed to sign on, the screen will fill with colors and graphics for Prodigy, AOL, and CompuServe (if you're using CompServe's graphical interface software), and lines of text on GEnie, Delphi, and CompuServe (if you're using the command line method, in which you type commands and see only words—no graphics—on screen). Each of these services offers a variety of information and entertainment-related

```
TERMINAL=

@c cris
CRIS CONNECTED
Welcome...


Welcome To CRIS!

ONLINE via X.25 AT 15:54 25-OCT-94

If you already have a User-ID on
CRIS, type it in and press RETURN.
Otherwise type "new"phyllis

Enter your password: *******

Greetings, Phyllis, welcome back to CRIS.

There is old mail in your mailbox!


<<HIT ANY KEY>> or Q to QUIT
Alt-Z FOR HELP | ANSI |       | FDX | 9600 N81 | LOG CLOSED | PRINT OFF | ON-LINE
```

Figure 1-1. *BBS Direct/CRIS BBS opening screen*

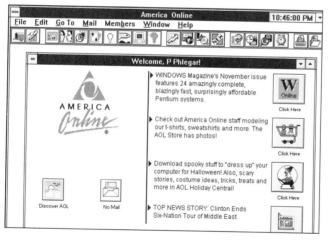

Figure 1-2. *America Online welcome screen*

forums and departments. As you navigate through these areas, you can read new postings and messages, create new postings for a particular topic, and send email to other frequenters of the forums—you can even check to see who is currently cruising the same place you are. Live chat sometimes looks like someone else is using your keyboard, because as somebody sends a message to you, it arrives on your screen almost instantaneously. It often feels as spontaneous and unpredictable as face-to-face conversation.

Cybersex May Be the Safest Kind of Sex

When these online conversations go on privately, they can get pretty hot and heavy. There are many people online—and you may be one of them—who enjoy a lively, uninhibited chat. And it is only logical that some conversations become sexually charged for the individuals involved. Quite often, the two people in this sort of exchange are hoping for a satisfying means to an end—this is computer sex. Described this way, it may sound strange or crude; but like sex IRL, the quality of cybersex depends on who's doing what to whom, how you feel about the other person(s) involved, and what you ultimately want out of the encounter.

There's no denying that love online is a strange and unexpected offshoot of technological achievement! Many new users of online services—especially women who use their identifiably female names—get on for the first time and find other members cruising them, asking personal questions, or even "hitting on them." This leads some people to believe that most online services and bulletin boards are just "sex networks." And yes, there is a lot of sexual chatter on the computer screen, taking a variety of forms, from forums devoted to alternative sexual interests and discussions, to casual meetings, electronic coffeehouses, or rendezvous in the virtual hot tubs found on some of your friendly national commercial services. (**Virtual** refers to a digital or electronic representation of an action on the computer screen.) Cybersex was almost bound to happen in this realm—particularly when you consider that it's the safest kind of sex.

You can't catch any diseases and you can't be seen or identified as the person you are IRL (provided you don't say too much about yourself). If someone's not into what you are, they can always avoid you, sign off, or tell you to go find a more willing partner.

HOW I FOUND LOVE ONLINE

The following story is particularly important to me and has everything to do with the writing of this book. Here's my husband sharing his story of love online:

"On July 2, 1991, I logged onto Prodigy, just like I did every night. I had been on Prodigy since the service began in Sacramento. I would spend hours each night in the "Computer Club" publicly answering questions about computer hardware and software. My marriage was on the rocks and this was the sum total of my social life.

A woman posted a question about the new DR-DOS version 5 (then a just-released computer operating system). Since I was familiar with the software, I answered (as did some others). A few days later she posted another question, and again, I answered. This went on for a couple of weeks. One day I signed on and my "email waiting" light flashed at me. Since I almost never received private mail (unless it was "junk mail" advertising something), I immediately checked to see what it was. It was a letter from the same woman, saying that she was embarrassed to appear so stupid publicly and could she ask me some more questions privately. I said of course she could—that was the reason I was there, to help people with computer problems. We traded messages pertaining to computers for a while, then sometime later she told me about her cat (a female named Saturn!) who had cancer. She was heartbroken because her companion of twelve years was going to die. I wrote back that I could empathize, since I had just lost my dog of fourteen *years only a few short months before. This was a turning point in our "relationship," and we began to talk about ourselves and I revealed some of my innermost thoughts and feelings I'd never told to anyone to this person I had never met!*

To make a long story short, over the next few months we began to open up to each other. She finally told me that she was an anchor on a national radio network that had an affiliate that I could hear in Sacramento. Once I heard her voice on the air, things changed for me—I can't begin to define it. The entity I was writing to on the computer suddenly became a living, breathing person. Then she wanted to hear my voice, but wasn't ready to talk to me yet. I gave her the phone number to my voice mail at work and told her when she could be reasonably sure that I wouldn't answer the phone. Funny though, the morning she chose to call, I was expecting a call from one of the investment brokers that I was doing business with and answered the phone. There was stunned silence for a few seconds, then she said "You're not supposed to be answering the phone!" We laughed and talked briefly and I could tell she wasn't too comfortable with it, so I kept it short and hoped that she wouldn't blow me off. She didn't, and we finally began talking on the phone and then exchanged pictures. In January 1992, we met for the first time. I was flying to Madison, Wisconsin, on a business trip and arranged to go through Denver. She met me at the airport. Talk about scared! After all these months, crazy as it sounded, I was already in love with this woman and now we were about to meet, face-to-face. What if she didn't find me attractive? What if I didn't find her attractive? What if.... To make a long story short, the meeting went well.

After this, the craziness began in earnest! We couldn't stand to be apart and came up with all kinds of creative ideas to get together. Once I drove for two days just to spend the weekend!

Eventually my divorce was final and my house in California was about to be sold. She and I already had bought a house in August 1992 in her town, and I packed everything into a U–Haul and drove out. We got married in January 1993."

Of course, if it were left to me, I would write a whole book on this story alone. But I thought better of that, and suffice to say, my husband has given you the really important stuff—except for one thing: my cat companion, Saturn, (who was supposed to die) is now fifteen years old. She's sitting on my lap as I write this, over three years later.

HOW THIS BOOK CAN HELP YOU

Remember, there was a time when I (and everyone who's online now) had no idea what cyberspace meant or what was out there in the online world. The goal of this book is to help you recognize both the pitfalls and the potential of loving online and how to make sure that cybersex really is safe sex, if that's what you plan to do. In Chapter Two, we will discuss issues, instructions, and advice for anyone seeking love online. This chapter cuts immediately to some facts of online life and gives practical information on exactly what you should and should not do, including how to make effective use of email while protecting your privacy; what to do if you want to take the relationship offline; the dangers of kids online and some precautions you can take with them, and more.

Chapter Three takes a hard and fast look at cybersex, hot chats, virtual hot tubs, private "rooms," and other assorted steamy online areas, as well as some actual transcripts of conversations, from which you can get a real sense of what's going on out there. Chapters Four, Five, and Six are guided tours of the hot spots for folks meeting up and hanging out on BBSs, the commercial services, and the Internet. I'll take you to the main areas of activity and give practical information on what to do and what not do to in order to get the most out of each forum or service; how to cruise for fun and friends, romance and racy chatting, or for cybersex. The Appendix gives general information on how to get connected, what you're going to need, numbers to call for service providers or commercial services, and other books on the subject of online communications, email, Internet, and so on.

Finding love online—what we think of as "true" love—is, just like IRL, pretty much a happy accident. It could happen for you, but it just as easily could not. I can't promise that after reading this book you'll go online and instantly meet your life's true love. But I do know that there are thousands of friendly, fascinating people online who you can talk to immediately. And they'll talk back.

CHAPTER TWO

▶

What You Need to Know
Before Going Online

Some people go online in a well-defined pattern or routine. They may spend time during the day cruising the Internet or hanging out on local BBSs or commercial services. Others come home from work and spend their leisure hours online at old familiar bulletin boards, chatting in real time with whomever happens to be there, or checking the postings and responding—or not—then heading off for new online terrain.

Still others may log on once a day, quickly retrieving the news and information of interest to them, while some people don't get cranking until after midnight on the adult BBSs, exchanging lively, interactive messages into the wee hours of the morning when the action starts to wind down. No matter what the profile, if you spend enough time online, it'll start to feel like your "other life," your online life.

The communication is electronic in that words are transmitted across wires to reappear on computer screens, but the experience and sensation of online life can become as real to you as physical life. All those words and messages and postings originated from someone at the other end of the line who has a physical presence. And so, while people have many different reasons for being online and many different ways of spending time there, everyone you meet in cyberspace is real.

GENERAL CAUTIONARY ADVICE

Online communication is a wonderful equalizer; everyone is communicating at the same level, and the flow of information from mind to mind gets pretty revealing at times. That's the beauty of talking to other people online: Even though some individuals choose to be deceptive, many others see the online world as the ultimate place in which to be totally honest because they feel safe enough to do so. If you're able to be honest online, you may come to understand yourself better as a result.

You'll find that as long as the person or people you are talking to can't trace you, free-flowing communication between strangers is very safe. However, if you plan to be a regular poster on a certain public board and would prefer not to get too personal too soon, plan to keep your thoughts in private email or to yourself until you feel more familiar with what goes on there.

Though this advice may seem like plain old common sense, even if you are the most savvy, sensible person in the world, you may let your guard down online, because being online *feels* different, as if the people you are talking to exist only in your monitor. You're probably sitting in familiar surroundings and feel safe and secure as you cruise new forums and meet dozens of new people. For this reason, it may seem that there is no need to protect yourself in the same way you naturally would offline.

For example, you're having a very honest conversation with someone hundreds of miles away; you may feel that you're just writing in a journal as opposed to actually sending messages to another live human being. You might reveal personal details that could lead, at the least, to annoying and invasive email, and at the worst, to someone showing up at your door unexpectedly. There is no reason to take chances by taking your personal safety for granted just because you're inside your home.

TAKE IT SLOW TO START

As I mentioned in Chapter One, some people online pretend to be something or someone that they are not in real life. What does it matter to you if someone is not who they say they are? It doesn't when being online is largely an exchange of information, like downloading files. But if you're feeling emotion about those people, thinking of them as friends or potential lovers, you'll want and need to know who it really is you're talking to, exchanging opinions with, and confiding in. If you want to meet someone online with whom you'll have a relationship of some substance, be it a friend, a playmate, or a life mate, don't be in a rush; you have to take the time to get the whole picture and get to know more about someone. Whether you've decided to be involved in one or several local boards or to go national with one of the larger services, you have a wealth of people to choose from, and your caution and thoughtfulness in getting to know who's who will pay off.

Honey, since when does falling in love take time? Here, it takes even LESS time than "out there!" You log on and talk for hours every night, and weeks pass in a matter of days. When words are all you have, you can go DEEP very fast, into your heart and soul. Deep into truth. Deep into lies.

—Poet, a BBS user

GETTING STARTED ONLINE

When I began my online life, the first places I went to were the **public messaging boards**, which are found on literally every national service and the local BBSs as well. Public messaging boards, also known as bulletin boards or forums, are a great place to *watch* what folks are up to and what they are interested in. On FidoNet and many bulletin board systems, these areas are called **echoes**. On the Internet, you can participate in discussion groups called **newsgroups**, and you can also subscribe to mailing lists and receive lots of new information through email messages on a particular topic.

Here are the steps I found helpful in the very beginning as I ventured online to the public messaging groups:

- Check out the areas that interest you—sports, knitting, sci-fi, and so on.
- Take the time to really read through the posts.
- Get to know who the regulars are.
- If you have no questions, there's no need to post any messages—yet.
- Look for messages that really catch your attention, reply if you feel like it, or continue to wait it out for a while.

Plenty of people cruise the postings without replying—it's known as **lurking**. There is no rule that says you should come out of lurk mode until you are ready. Lurking is not unlike sitting on your front porch, watching the neighbors go by, or going to the mall or city to people-watch. You're just checking things out and taking information in.

When I first decided to go "public" and start communicating with the online world, I posted a question to ALL on a public messaging area on a national online service. A public message is different from a private message—everyone can read it, as opposed to a private message addressed to only one person. The question I posted publicly was about the operating system used by the man who was to become my husband. He was replying to a lot of messages, but not all of them, and my message struck a chord with him, so he answered back. I wasn't conscious of it at the moment, but his notes also got my attention.

My messages pertained to the computer-related topic we were currently discussing as a group, and I avoided including anything personal; this is really the best approach when you are new to an area on one of the boards.

Despite experiencing some episodes where the reality of actually meeting someone didn't live up to their online potential, I have met some really nice guys online. An interesting thing about communicating online is that it seems easier to get to know the men who are farther away. When I would get a response from someone who is local, immediately we'd take the friendship to the phone, then in person—so we would lose the advantage of really getting to know the person better through their letters before that first meeting. The guys far away are the ones who have actually become friends.
—Marie, a Prodigy user

Going online provides the gay man and woman an additional option for meeting new people. We usually don't have the advantage of meeting at work or through other "traditional" ways. We either have bookstores, bars, or friends. The bars and bookstores are not for everyone; therefore the computer is a great alternative. It allows us to chat, check out vital stats, such as drinking, smoking and even sexual habits. It basically can be used as a dating service, a social club, or just an outlet to alleviate stress.

What I would like to say to the straight people online, about gays online, is that of course we are out there. Be respectful, and if the opportunity arises, talk to us, learn about us and stop fearing us. Most gay people are not out for sex... we are just people who want to live, love, and be loved, and have the same opportunities as anyone else. You know, the American Dream, living with the one we love in the house on a quiet little street with a white picket fence, the dog in the front yard and the barbeque grill in the backyard. We are simply people trying to live our lives to the fullest, like you.
—Assistant Sysop of a Gay and Lesbian BBS

PROTECT YOUR PRIVACY

As you venture forth in the online world, remember that the online attitude and persona you display contributes toward others' perceptions of you and therefore your safety. Consider advice you may have been given about walking through an unknown part of a city—look like you know what your destination is and walk like you know where you're going. Finding out how to express yourself in the way that works best for you might take a little while; as you're learning the ropes, at least be aware of some things you should reveal slowly, if ever:

- your physical address
- your telephone number
- the fact that you live alone
- where you work
- any financial information about yourself

There is no need to immediately divulge your marital status. Keep in mind, however, that in some forums people (of the opposite sex) may ignore you unless they believe you are available. If people think you're married, you're apt to meet far fewer people who are looking for romance.

You should be yourself online, but you should also try to cultivate a voice that projects confidence and savviness. It's okay to say, "I'm new to this service and I'd welcome some help" but don't say something like, "Oh, I wish I could meet someone, it gets so lonely sometimes," or "Gosh, I just get so depressed every now and then." Expressing this type of sentiment online is like having a "kick me" sign on your back. If you need to express these feelings, do it in a forum where your ID is not visible. Your ID is your online name, the name the system recognizes you by when you sign on; your ID also shows when you post publicly and in email.) If you're expressing something of a truly personal nature, do it where you can use a special "handle" or alias, used often on some of the adult, explicit chat forums on the national services. Otherwise, you may be easy prey for a manipulative person who might want to lure you into a relationship to embezzle money from you, or perhaps to meet you IRL for sex—or who knows what. You probably know what police say about safety in your house: Crooks can break in if they really want to, but they are going to focus on the easy targets. The same is true online. People can find out anything they want about anybody if they try hard enough, but the last thing you want to do is come across online as vulnerable. Keeping personal information to yourself goes a long way to protecting you.

Pay very close attention to what someone asks you, and think before you respond. Just a few details about your geography and a mention or two about your activities—such as going to ball games at particular stadiums—and you've given away more information than you probably meant to. For example, if you're less than a day's drive from the coast and go to Braves games, it's a good bet that you are near Atlanta. People have been known to use tricks such as saying, "Seems I remember your telling me you were near the Capitol" to get you to say, "Oh no, I said the Empire State Building." Concentrate on maintaining your anonymity early in a relationship (while building trust) and follow these tips.

- Don't advertise your material belongings or financial gains.
- Don't talk about your financial situation, or even your job if it will give the impression that you have something worth taking.
- Don't ever let anyone have your password for any reason. Once someone goes online on your ID, they

can read your private mail and send mail and post messages in your name.
- Watch out for victimizers who come on like they are vulnerable and needy.

A well–known con artist line is "I'm dying and alone." There have been a few cases of people claiming to be terminal from one disease or another, which they use as a ploy to manipulate kind, sympathetic people. Sadly, it makes life very tough for those who are truly in need of help. However, if someone you meet online claims to be dying of AIDS, for example, consider donating money in that person's name to a local AIDS assistance program or hospice. To save yourself from unscrupulous people, keep the following advice in mind.

- Do not ever send anyone money.
- Don't send gifts, unless you are part of a group that regularly does swaps.
- Don't accept collect calls.

Member Lists

Whether you're online locally or nationally, there is usually a member list. On some services you're automatically "enrolled" and on others, you have to make a request to be put on the list; some have online bios that you can write yourself.

These member lists and their bios are handy because you can use them to search for someone by name (for example, an old friend you've lost touch with). A member list usually contains your name, city, state, and system ID. Some services allow you to write and add your bio. Decide for yourself if you want to be included on the member list. You can leave out your location and last name (or delete yourself from the list altogether) if you are worried about giving your fellow subscribers too much information. See Chapter Four for more information on bios.

Additional Security Measures

You may want to take further measures to help guarantee your safety. The following are simply suggestions; most people don't go to this extreme, but should you desire to, the option is available.

- Consider signing on to a service using another name.
- Get a shielded P.O. box (in which the mail that arrives at the box is sent to yet another address—either another regular box or your house).
- Get an unlisted number.

Screennames

What **user name**, nickname, handle, or alias you choose helps keep the wolves away, too (or attract them); if your nickname is Bambi or Hot Stud, you will probably attract the attention of people who are looking for hot chat. If your goal is to make some platonic contacts initially, don't choose an obviously gender-specific name. If you're hoping for sexually charged contacts right away, gear your nickname in that direction.

While online one night, I couldn't resist sending a message to a person whose nickname was Hard Reed. I asked him if he played the clarinet or oboe. He said that, in fact, he did. One shouldn't make assumptions, but I'd imagine this person to be aware of the sexual "overtones" in such a name!

CYBERSEX MIND GAMES

It's complicated when you meet someone who might become a serious romantic partner in an adult, graphic sex-talk or **hot chat** area. In part, it's an issue of trust—the fact that you met in the hot chat "playpen" may imprint and have an impact on any other kind of relationship you try to have with that person later on. Consider this: You meet, have cybersex with someone who then claims to want more out of the relationship with you. If you later find that person in the hot chat area, you might wonder if he or she is fooling around. And would you want a real-life relationship with a person who instantly—and constantly—wants to "play" on that level? As IRL, meeting someone in a common interest forum and letting the relationship grow for a while without any sexual slant to it may be a better method for developing a serious relationship.

Also, don't confuse someone's interest in computer sex with you as anything more than a one-night stand in the cyberworld, even if you meet with the same individual over a long period of time. Your cybermate may say a lot of serious-sounding things, but unless they want to talk about something else besides sex, don't expect anything further.

WHAT DO YOU LOOK LIKE?

There is an old joke told among veteran cybersex surfers: No matter what they tell you about themselves physically, add ten years, forty pounds, and take off three inches on ANY measurement where bigger is better. Not everyone is lying, of course. When it appears your relationship with someone online will become physical, you'll both want to know what the other looks like—a really good argument for being truthful from the outset.

I corresponded online with my future husband for months before knowing how old he was or what he looked like. When it seemed possible that we might meet in person, we started talking about our physical appearance and eventually exchanged pictures. I've also attended conferences where everyone in the room is part of an online club, and we all had on name tags. It was exciting to know who was who, not because looks were that important, but all the time we had each spent online without being able to see or speak with each other made the first face-to-face meeting more exciting than a typical first-time introduction.

In many cases, people exaggerate their looks online, only telling the truth after a few phone conversations and exchanging pictures with someone. Sometimes these people just want to feel beautiful or avoid the issue of appearance entirely; after all, in cyberspace one's physical being is essentially irrelevant. For those hoping that their cyberromps would go as far as sex IRL, the real deal on their physical appearance would be...exposed.

A teenager I met online once said, "When hearing and sight are gone from the interaction, it becomes a mental process on both sides of the screen." I think lying about how you look or anything else about yourself is not a good idea, but you don't have to tell all, or anything, if you don't want to. You have the right to be online for that mental process and nothing else.

Sometimes you can be very specific about how you look and still surprise someone. One friend I'd met told me he didn't look his age, but when I did meet him, I was surprised that he did in fact look so much younger than he was. A very intense and extended mental connection with someone can make actually meeting the person face-to-face a bit disorienting—they may still not look like you imagined, even though they told you exactly what they looked like.

One thing about meeting people online that I think is a big plus is being able to control the image I project. Some guys are intimidated by women who are successful, independent, and intelligent. On the computer, I can control how I come across and maybe get some guys to think twice about me, even if I'm the sort of person they wouldn't normally be drawn to in real life. I don't mean to sound manipula-

tive, but I do have a little more leeway in choosing what I want to disclose about myself when I'm sitting here at my computer. I can take my time at getting to know someone. I use common sense. I don't believe everything I read on the computer and I look for little things that give me clues. For example, I look for people who are articulate and can spell!
—Marie, a Prodigy user

THE QUESTION OF IDENTITY

For whatever reason, some people take on the identity of someone of the opposite gender. In most cases of gender switching it is men assuming women's identities. A simple explanation for this might be that there are a lot more men online than women, but the real reasons are probably far more complex. Gender switching is common online, so be sure to ask a few questions first. If you are not looking for friends but for sex and have any doubts as to whether or not you're talking to someone of the gender you prefer, go on to someone else. It's easy to get your potential cybersex partner to talk a little about his or her sexual preferences, desires, and fantasies, and this should help you to determine whether or not you are talking to the gender you prefer.

In person or online, men and woman have different ways of talking when it comes to sex. Men tend to be more direct than women, but many men won't notice or care how blunt the supposed female they are chatting with may be—in fact, they may like it and forget to consider the fact this she could be a he. No matter how many specific and probing questions you ask, if a gender-switcher is very good at deception, it may be difficult to expose the truth. Sometimes you have to let your instincts guide you.

MAKING YOUR MOTIVES CLEAR

Many people don't take sexy chatting very seriously, and there is always a danger you or someone you're flirting with will read more into an online flirtation or recurring sexual liaison than is actually there. Here are some simple rules to follow to help prevent confusion and misunderstanding:

- Make your motives as clear as you can. Do you have real feelings about this person, or is it just computer sex?
- Don't talk about the future if there really isn't any chance that the online relationship will become something IRL.
- Don't tell anyone how important they are, unless you really do want the relationship to get serious.
- While chatting online, don't talk about and compare your real-life loves (husband, wife, girlfriend, boyfriend) with your computer "love."

It's one thing to say you're online either because your partner doesn't have sex with you often enough or won't do kinky things with you; it's quite another to start making comparisons that might make your cybersex partner think that you are looking for something more permanent. If things are moving along too quickly for you in any situation, romantic or not, don't hesitate—just say no. You don't have to answer any questions that make you uncomfortable or write back to anyone you're not interested in.

ADDICTED TO CYBERLOVE

Watch your accrued time online and assess how you feel about your activities; are you becoming obsessed with being online? There are lots of people to choose from online—a new sex partner can be found instantly at any time. Cybersex with lots of people can be addictive. Online sexual stimulation seems very safe, not unlike reading adult magazines and fantasizing about the naked women or men. Without realizing it, you can get carried away. Married people who go online might say that they are neither having real affairs nor short-changing their mates. However, anyone truly addicted to computer sex won't be looking at their behavior rationally and may do serious damage to their marriage without realizing it. It can also get very expensive—people addicted to chatting may spend hours online each night.

A fascination with the online world is normal for the first several weeks or even months, but if you start forsaking all other regular activities and people in your life for your friends online, you may be addicted. I've heard horror stories of people who hang out in the live chat and adult chat areas for hours every night, running up huge bills and eventually going broke. When BBSs and online services go out of business, it has not been unheard of for some users to become very depressed, and even suicidal—a worst case scenario, but more common than you might imagine. There is a difference between addiction and the fascination of going online frequently when you've just gotten your computer and modem and it all feels very new. It's reasonable to expect that at first you'll spend a lot of your spare time (or work time, in many cases) in search of the next amorous adventure. Your perception will change as you spend more time online and get more familiar with the medium. If you keep your perspective and maintain a balance between your offline and online activities, your chances of getting what you want out of online communications improve greatly.

Consider the story of Marilyn, whose husband has become very close to a woman who he's been writing to online. Neither one of them were especially knowledgeable about online communications when they first signed up for one of the national services.

When my husband Tom and I first signed onto our service, our eyes just about popped out of our heads when we realized how most people were using this service. We had both heard about people meeting over the Internet and jokes about cybersex, but we had no idea how big the service was or how explicit the people using it really were. At first we laughed and joined in a little bit, and it was fun. I soon grew tired of it, though. Tom kept at it, and as days went by I realized he was spending up to three hours a night online. He never hid anything from me though, so I was able to see what he was saying to any of the number of women he was "chatting" with whenever I walked into the room. To Tom, and to me, it was all in good fun and nothing to be taken seriously. I never felt the least bit jealous or threatened, because it all seemed slightly ridiculous. We've been married for four years, and I've never had any reason to doubt Tom's loyalty to me. Also, I've always believed that we all have secret selves, parts of us that fantasize about sex with other people—and that it's OK, as long as you don't act on those fantasies. So I let him have his fun because to me it actually felt safe—I knew that if Tom had this secret sexual self (as I do), then I'd rather he was in the next room typing on a computer than out with another woman. This went on for about a month.

Then one morning he got up and, not ashamedly but sort of warily, told me that he'd been talking to a woman until 2:00 a.m. the night before. A woman who is married to a man who's (allegedly) heavily involved in illegal activities. She described her life in detail, telling of how she feels like a prisoner in her own home and said that because of her husband's lifestyle, she must have bodyguards with her at all times and cannot ever go anywhere alone. She spends most days alone with few friends, no family, and little to do except talk on the computer. She refuses to give any information about where she lives (not even the state). She does not respond to any questions that might lead to a clue about where she lives. Tom seemed obsessed with this woman. As someone who has worked in a life-saving profession, his first instinct is to "save" people, and this woman was crying out to be saved. Unlike the other women he flirted with, this woman was more real, more human. She had a haunting personality and a dark mysteriousness. It was easy to envision this young, beautiful woman being held prisoner by her husband, so sad and alone. Tom was hooked. He tried to verify her story by quizzing some of the other people, men and women, in the room. They all said that she had been in their group for a long time and that she did not flirt the way the other women did. She was almost always depressed. She seemed to only just want someone to talk to. He continues to talk to her about every other day, for long periods.

So far, this relationship between them has not had any effect on our marriage, and he continues to tell me about their conversations. But somehow I now realize that there is a danger here that one's emotions can become involved and this "game" can become far more serious. My faith in Tom has not yet been shaken, but I now have a healthy respect for the power of these online relationships.

I have not asked Tom to stop conversing with this woman because I know he can't stop, yet. He would feel as if he were abandoning

her. I trust him to know where the boundaries are and to end their online relationship if and when he feels the lines are about to be crossed. So, the saga continues.
—Marilyn, a member of one of the national services

Tom did try to check on the woman's story, but the resources available to him for verification weren't much, outside the help of other subscribers. Who really knows if this person was revealing the truth or weaving some grand tale of mystery and intrigue? There are some things you can do to check up on identity and stories, but just as often you're going only on a hunch and your intuition. Our natural inclination to believe rather than doubt others can sometimes make for a difficult job of sorting out the cranks and flakes from the truthful or the truly needy. Your detection skills will improve with care and practice, but some people will still fool you; I don't think it's humanly possible to always know who is for real and who is not. I still get fooled. It's your ability to give up, to cut off communications, and go on that will keep things moving along positively for you.

EXPOSING AND AVOIDING DECEPTION

One of the hardest things to accept about chatting online is that someone may be deceiving you. If you want to learn more about an online interest, consider getting a second ID and sitting back and watching how potential partners treat the "other" you. (Admittedly, this method is itself deceitful. I suggest it only as a possibility; such sleuthing may not be your style.) Don't try and deceive someone who is seriously looking for a relationship; just see if the person you're interested in tells your other persona the same things you've been told once.

This is a good way to check out the stories your love interest is telling, as is lurking for their public messages (if you don't know, ask them what forums they frequent) over a two- or three-month period. You'd be surprised what you can discover. The gender-switcher can also be exposed by that same technique. My husband and I, on separate computers with our own gender-specific IDs, were hit on by the same person who told me "he" was a man and told my husband "she" was a woman.

In the live chat or adult hot chat areas, deception is not uncommon, and this double-identity method can help you work out who's being honest and who's not. There is no need to keep up your double life or get a second computer; just use the duality sparingly to ensure you're not getting the runaround. The majority of people online are good folks; it's just the occasional rotten apples that make it necessary for you to be cautious.

You can also use your other acquaintances online as sources of information about a person you're interested in. If others online know your potential mate offline, ask them casually what they know about him or her; casual questions such as, "Are they as nice IRL as they seem online?" can lead to new and useful information.

IF YOU TAKE IT OFFLINE

There are lots of ways to find out more about anyone you are interested in getting to know better online, especially if you feel you may want to meet them f2f. Here are some key points about moving a relationship forward:

- Read the person's public posts and observe how she/he relates to everyone.
- If she/he seems somehow defensive, negative, overly

"instructional," or short-tempered, you should probably avoid her/him.
- Lurking and observing what they say and reveal about themselves for a few weeks will allow you to see their personality.

Deciding whether or not to take it offline can be a pivitol point in your relationship with your potential friend or mate; once you've met in person, that particular emotional connection of "online only" will be changed forever. The relationship might be better, with luck, and it will certainly be different—but you'll never have the mystery of just words on the screen again. Take your time in moving toward meeting someone in person.

Once you've decided it's the right thing to do, meeting in person needs to be planned out. Keep the following guidelines in mind as you make your arrangements.

- The first face-to-face needs to be in a very public place.
- You might plan the meeting as an activity that involves your friends.
- Don't have your computer friend stay with you in your home.
- Arrange for a hotel room for whomever is the visitor during a planned meeting.
- Meet in sexually neutral places such as shopping malls, restaurants, or museums.
- Don't put yourself in the position of being trapped alone with this person.
- Don't commit to anything that you might regret.

No amount of chatting online can prepare you for the actual personal encounter; some people, despite their on-screen sexual bravado, may never be able to or want to make the leap to physical sex because of a lack of physical chemistry, real-world awkwardness, just plain fear, or something else.

KIDS ONLINE

Because computers are in many homes, and a lot of kids know how to use those computers better than do their parents, an inevitable online issue becomes kids going places and doing things in cyberspace they probably shouldn't. Unless you're using an online service that offers a "parental control" feature, there's no way—other than constant supervision—to prevent children from cruising the "adults only" areas and interacting with people they meet along the way. At the very least, it leads to disillusionment or disappointment for one or both parties, and at the worst, inadvertent child abuse. Imagine if the seemingly shy and sweet woman in the adult hot chat area turns out to be twelve years old.

One way to avoid such a scenario is asking a few key questions.

- What do you do for a living?
- What kind of car do you drive?
- When were you born and where?
  How has that part of the country changed in your opinion?
- Have you traveled much, and where?
- What did you do while you were traveling?
- What is your favorite part of the country?
- What's the standard of living like where you are now?
- How hard was it for you to find your apartment/buy your house?

If you examine their responses and go just a step further with your queries, it will be tough for most kids to keep up the front as an adult for very long. For example, if someone tells you they were born in the late 1940s, you could ask them about the cars they drove in high school, how they felt about Vietnam, and so on.

Other likely kid indicators are bad spelling, overly eager responses, and expressions of "clinginess" or over-dependency on new cyberfriends. There have been a few TV situtation comedies with story lines about kids having an online romance with an adult. When the ruse was discovered, the show made light of the situation. What they didn't mention was the likely discomfort that occurred for the adult who discovered that this cybersex lover was a child. It goes without saying that being spoken to in a sexual way, even without an immediate physical factor, is absolutely not a healthy situation for any young person. The bottom line is that parents must watch their children's activities online and block their access to adult areas whenever possible, and you must be cautious.

YOUR PERSONAL GROWTH ONLINE

Going online and becoming part of cyberspace will change you. In fact, it can be a life-altering experience. It gives you more opportunities to meet people, seek information, express yourself, and discover new ways to have sex or make love. You may get a new take on what you think is attractive or desirable in a person. Understanding the consequences of online communications and knowing what some of the likely outcomes can be will help you get the most out of your trip to cyberspace.

CHAPTER THREE

▶

Hot Chats and Hot Tubs:
Advice for the Interested

> *There is no sex online, and you couldn't fax each other a cigarette afterwards even if there was."*
> —Jack Rickard, Editor/Publisher,
>   Boardwatch Magazine, *July 1994*

Jack is right, of course. There are a lot of things you can do online, but obviously sex can't actually take place on a computer. Not yet, anyway. What *is* happening online is sexual activity—the swapping of messages between two or more people with the intention of both parties being aroused to their mutual satisfaction. Cybersex is solitary sexual self-stimulation on some levels, but there is a very important difference. The interaction is more than just reading a magazine with erotic words and images. The words on your screen are from a live, breathing (make that heavy breathing) human at the other end of the connection. It's even more compelling than phone sex, because with cybersex, your partner has got you *by the brains*!

On the national services, you can control the kind of input you want by not talking about anything or to anyone you don't want to. Most live chat areas provide possibilities for sex and/or romance, depending on what you write in your bio. If you say something like, "Hi, I'm looking for friends and maybe something romantic; no hot chat, please," you probably won't be bothered by a lot of people who want hot chat. If your bio says "Hi, my tongue is on fire, talk to me, quench me," then expect a lot of attention from people with sex and only sex on their minds.

On CompuServe, the CB Simulator (as in CB radio) chat area is probably the place where the first cyberspace romance blossomed in the '80s. Today, the need for a meeting place for socially and sexually minded folks is specifically addressed by America Online, a service that named its live chat area People Connection, which stays filled with folks looking for literally everything from a casual flirtation to sex in a virtual hot tub. Live, private chat for any and all reasons is available on all the national services. Some of the people who go to the live chat areas are just curious about what goes on there; some are lonely. Others want a mind-slamming sexual fantasy, possibly to fill a few gaps in their social lives or to replace real sex in a world of sexually transmitted diseases. *Not all people get involved exclusively for sex, but they sometimes become progressively more involved in sex after meeting someone they're interested in.*

There are many places to go in the online world if you're looking for sex or romance. There are local BBSs that try for a more romantic theme catering to singles looking for a mate. One such BBS is "Lonely Heart" with private email and public forums with regular get-togethers that allow members to meet each other in person. Then there are the BBSs like "Percy's Playhouse" with files full of hard-core pictures catering to all adult sexual proclivities as well as live chat, hot enough to make you consider the strength of the insulation on your phone lines!

If you would like access to an adult BBS, be prepared to send the sysop some proof of age. The sysop will be the only person who will know your real name (most adult BBSs and adult areas have the option for user nicknames or aliases) and your address. Often, applications for admission to adult areas are available for downloading. Here is an example of what part of an application could look like:

APPLICATION FOR ACCESS TO THE ADULT AREAS ON PERCY'S PLAYHOUSE

Please read, fill out completely, sign, provide proof of age (photocopy of a valid drivers license, state ID, military ID, birth certificate,

passport, or other similar evidence), and mail to:
Percy c/o Percy's Playhouse
P.O. Box 555
Anytown, USA 55555

As soon as this form is received and found satisfactory, access to adult areas will be granted. Your signature on the bottom signifies that you will not provide your password or download any adult files to anyone under the age of 18.

After I mentioned that I was writing this book, the sysop of a local adult-oriented BBS ("Colorado Schwings") asked if I'd like my own special adult area called Pink's Corner. (My nickname/alias online was Pink.) This special area was for adults only and had public but no private message capabilities. Consequently participants would be sharing their thoughts with the group or with whomever was lurking. Pink's Corner gave me an opportunity to conduct frank, running conversations about members' sexual activity online, either on Colorado Schwings or somewhere else. Furthermore, having my own adult area allowed me to get to know the range of people interested in cybersex and to hear some of their experiences. The sysop got things started by sending messages to all the people who had access to the adult area, inviting them to check out my corner. When I first logged on as Pink, there were several messages waiting and people were chatting among themselves. A message from Virgie got things heated up right off the bat:

From: VIRGIE
To: PINK

It's like this, Pink, I'm really into erotic images. I love oil, hot, wet, slick, and dribbling down your back. I watch it pool in the small of your back. I rub it up to your shoulder blades, my hands cupping your back and rubbing you deeply. You drop your head towards the pillow, your hair falling forward revealing the nape of your neck. My hand runs quickly up your spine, moving easily on your exposed flesh, the feel of the warm oil sending shivers up your body. I dig in to your flesh with my strong fingers and pull the tension away from your head, releasing a strong sigh of relief from your throat. The warm oil flows....Pink; it's been fun. More later...SIGH.

Virgie's message served as a good opener for some hot chatting. Anyone could have jumped in and continued the story. Another way to get familiar with your fellow chatter is through sharing fantasies or erotic storytelling. Here's what Dark had to say about it:

From: DARK
To: PINK
Dear Pink,
It is through my writing of stories on the boards that I flirt. Have I ever written stories for someone I love? OF COURSE! Some of them are as mild as French vanilla ice cream. Some of them have been hotter than Texas chili. But all of them are written with love and care.
To really write a story, you have to put a part of yourself into it. Otherwise, it is just a lump of lifeless clay. Have you ever been able to write a story that *did not* reveal something about you?

Here's what two other visitors to Pink's corner had to say about cybersex and why it works for them:

From: LEN
To: PINK
Re: ONLINE SEX
Modem sex has been known to turn me on. But it's kind of like reading a really hot adult book—a lot depends on who the writer is. You don't need to be bogged down by rules for modem sex—it's just like talking each other up on the phone, but a bit slower and more impersonal.

As far as sex with people I meet—well, it kind of depends on the person and the impression I get. What kind of sex? Well, I am pretty open to anything at least once <grin>.

From : Pink
To : LEN
Title: Re: ONLINE SEX

I am personally not that interested in modem sex for myself, but I can think of some situations where it's a good solution for those involved. For example, because you are homebound, you might use the computer as your nightly "watering hole" instead of going down to the corner bar. You have sexual needs, and while you'd prefer a relationship with someone you care for and have good sex with, you might find that modem sex is better than nothing; on occasion, it's better than solo sex because a real live person is at the other end.

A member of a national service had this to say about cybersex: "*Cybersex is cheap, surface level. (This is my opinion, ya understand!) I'm not saying cybersex isn't exciting especially at first, but I AM saying that rarely do you meet people who can really type well enough to KEEP the conversation exciting! I think one person usually entertains and the other gets something—mental or physical arousal—from the sexual-textual exchange. Sometimes a person will return the favor and entertain you, but usually they are instantly gone. There is a whole spectrum of sex in cyberspace, from the hard-core variety to "making love."*

When people talk about computer sex, either in person or on paper, it may seem ludicrous to the uninitiated. How could people get so worked up about text on a computer screen, after all? But keep in mind that although cybersex can't be compared with real-life sex, it has had a powerful effect on many people in cyberspace.

There are obviously a lot of things that take place in cyberspace that become difficult to define or quantify by real-life standards. Infidelity—and the debate as to just where computer sex crosses the lines of our real relationships—is one such concept.

IS IT INFIDELITY IF IT'S NOT "PHYSICAL"?

The fact that computer sex is happening only on screen can seem so harmless that suddenly you find yourself deeply involved with someone emotionally and unprepared to deal with it. Keep a close eye on yourself if you can, and if you think that you are getting too involved with someone, stand back from the situation and examine it. The following true story was emailed to me from Joe, a member of a national service, after he read my articles in *Boardwatch Magazine* on cyber-infidelity.

"At first I got into cybersex out of curiosity. I was not prepared for how powerful an experience it would be for me. I only connected with one person, and for a time we were pretty hot and heavy. We have now become very good friends. (At my request, we eliminated the cybersex from our relationship.) We are both married, and when I first got into the cybersex relationship, I was surprised at how compelling an experience it was. I was also upset with myself for getting into it. I couldn't figure out why I was getting so involved with someone through a computer. And I guess I rationalized that because it was through a computer it was not like a full-blown affair in 3D. But that rationalization collapsed when I realized I was becoming more interested in my friend than in my marriage."

The search for romantic or sexual excitement outside of any relationship obviously indicates potential problems. When cyberspace and its sexual arenas start to become more of an attraction than your partner, you might want to consider Joe's situation and learn from it.

"What I soon realized was that I had some very significant marital problems and that the online relationship was a symptom of that. My wife and I had started marital therapy about a month before I started the online relationship, and things really started heating up in our marital therapy after I realized what I was doing and why. It all culminated when I came close to moving out (I went so far as to put a deposit on an apartment). That simple act ended up helping both my wife and me to really face what was going on with us and understand how deep our attachment was to one another. I then took a weekend for myself to sort things out and get clearer on what I wanted.

I next contacted my online friend and we both agreed to keep the cybersex out of our relationship. (Coincidentally, while I was out of town she had confronted her husband with her own issues.) As a consequence of all of this, we both have improved primary relationships, if you can believe that! We have since settled into a nice email and occasional chat kind of thing, and it's been great—more of a support system than anything else."

Joe's story might seem like a typical one—an affair that ended up forcing a marriage to grow—until you consider that the "affair" took place over the computer! And he (like others in the online community) sees that the odd realism one can experience in an online relationship can be effective on a number of levels:

"I think that cybersex and online interaction is a new frontier for relationships. One of the things I struggled with, though, was not knowing what the rules were. At times it didn't seem quite real—like it was a holodeck fantasy (from Star Trek—for those in the know :)) or a journal that talks back to you. But part of me knew there was a real human being on the other end. My friend and I sorted out all kinds of issues that came up as a result of the "affair,"

but that was because both of us were willing to do so. I do believe that for a married person cybersex, on more than an experimental basis, is a symptom of marital problems, but perhaps an earlier symptom than a full-blown affair in 3D. It is a warning that something is not right here."

CYBERSEX AND SINGLES

Cybersex among singles is a bit different. When single people are online, choosing to hang out in adult areas of BBSs and similar places, concern that cybersex is in any way adulterous or indicative of marital problems isn't an issue. Here is how one woman put it:

"When I was first transferred to this city, I didn't know anyone except the people I worked with. It was a relatively small office and the men my age were all married, and the single men were either too young or not what I'd consider dating material. I was not interested in having an affair just for sex with anyone, nor was I comfortable with the idea of getting involved with anyone so soon. Besides, my co-workers already had lives when I got there.

I had left behind a comfortable relationship that I'd been in for years. He wasn't interested in anything permanent, and neither was I. Frankly, my biggest need was for sex. I've never been the sort of person who was into reading romance novels and getting turned on by that. It's always a real person I have to focus on whether or not I am with a partner. Going online not only took care of that—with cybersex—but also gave me a built-in social club, without any obligations or complications.

Time passed, and I grew roots and became part of a real life social circle and had a few boyfriends in the physical. In between the move and now, the computer's huge social circle of casual cybersex lovers served me quite well. I got what I needed in a no-strings, no-obligations way and it kept me from possibly having an affair at work, which I didn't really want to do. It would have been out of desperation, the desperation of the new girl in town who was understandably lonely and sexually frustrated.

Even now, I like to get online and have a chat and maybe computer sex, too. I like the freedom and control of the situation that I have through the computer. It gives me another choice, socially, for what I want to do on a Saturday night. Sometimes I prefer the simplicity."

CASUAL SEX AFICIONADOS GO ONLINE

The spread of AIDS and other sexually transmitted diseases has caused a distinct shift in behavior patterns for many people who would have sought casual sexual contact. The popularity of male and female strip clubs and 900 phone-sex lines seems to indicate that there are fewer people having casual sex and more people fantasizing about it. Perhaps the middle ground in that shift is computer sex. While no one would argue that it can replace real sex, those who enjoy it agree that computer sex is much better than a solo fantasy.

A recently separated man had this to say about computer sex:

"*Someone had recommended the online service, and I had signed on and subscribed out of curiosity. The only other online service I knew anything about was merely a bulletin board: there was no "live chat" capability.*

When I "stumbled" into the adult area, I found men and women there waiting to talk. I took it slowly at first—it was hard to believe that it was possible to have sex online. With women I'd never met! How could it be better than that? No complications; no involvements; no expectations other than what appeared on the screen. And there was no question that what I typed onto the screen was causing a reaction on the other end of the phone line. That reaction, and the fact that I could cause it to happen, was much different than reading a magazine with someone else's experiences or fantasies.

I was recently divorced and lonely. I had been married so long I didn't know how to date anymore, and I was scared of the dangers of sexually transmitted diseases. The meat markets were not my style anyway. I didn't feel good about becoming involved with anyone I worked with, and so I was left few choices. "Cybersex" seemed both safe and available, at any time of day or night. And because I didn't need or want any involvements at the time, it seemed the perfect solution.

My first online sexual experience astounded me. I couldn't believe it was actually happening. She was hot, and needed me as much as I needed her, and she was honest about it. Here was a woman who wanted the same thing I did. No pretentions, no excuses, no games being played. She wanted sex, just as I did. She wanted to feel desired and desirable, just as I did. She was explicit. We described what we would like to do with each other; how we would do it; what we liked.

It was apparent that she'd done this before—I was the novice. But it didn't take me long to get into making love via a keyboard and monitor. All I had to do, I found, was to write about what I would do, what I wanted to do. Her excitement aroused me, and the more turned on she got, the more excited I got.

"Tell me what you're doing right now," I said to her. She did. She described what she was wearing, how she was sitting, what she was doing to herself as we exchanged messages back and forth. I did the same. We "interacted," each of us alone on our sides of the monitor, but connected by the messages we transmitted to each other.

In the days that followed, I was obsessed. I had trouble concentrating at work. I thought about the next time we could be together in cyberspace. Could I really be this excited about a woman I'd "virtually" met? Well, truth was, the virtual reality of what we had done together had a much greater impact on me than I expected it might. It had actually felt good.

We met online often over the next few weeks. Sometimes when I would sign on, she wouldn't be there. Sitting there, in the adult "room," I struck up conversations with other women who were there, to take up time. On occasion, the conversations went further. So I became a cyberstud, making love to whomever would respond.

It was unbelievable! Different women constantly. Different sizes and shapes (if their descriptions of themselves were to be believed, and I did believe, unquestioningly, because I wanted to believe) and marital status, and occupations and ages. Many were married, simply not getting the attention or caring they needed in their marriages and looking for the companionship online that was missing in their daily lives. It didn't matter. In cyberspace, everyone is equal. Anyone can be exactly what they want to be—or you want them to be.

The anonymity of computer nicknames and the fact that none of us ever saw each other meant that we could say things that we never would have said had we met in person. Subjects that would have taken months to come up in conversation IRL were broached immediately in cyberspace. There was no need for embarrassment—no one could see anyone else blushing. I could say anything I wanted to someone I didn't really know, and if she didn't like it, so what? She could stop talking with me, and it didn't matter. There was always someone else."

When it comes to sex, there are more opinions than there are participants, and computer sex is no exception. Another onliner had this to say about cybersex:

"My opinion is that cybersex is a "beginners" phenomenon. Now there could be (probably are) some die-hard folks who continue to engage in cybersex for years, but I think for most people it is something they do in the beginning and perhaps deny later that they ever did! They tire of it quickly and move on to other things. I don't know

if this is different for women than for men. But I think that most of the people who find cybersex the only attraction to an online service tire of the service and drop it. But I think everyone who spends any time online tries cybersex at one time or another."

RULES OF THE CYBERSEX GAME

The following are some important tips you should be aware of if you're considering cruising for sex and love. In my many hours in the online chat areas talking to people about writing this book, I've heard this advice offered by those who are truly in the know.

Assume Nothing

You're better off asking than assuming when it comes to online relationships, even when things seem perfectly obvious. It's better to ask than to be disappointed, or worse, unpleasantly surprised.

Even in Cyberspace, People Are People

Jealousy, lying, manipulation, gossip, deception—all these and more are part of cyberspace, just as they, unfortunately, are part of real life. Of course, so are their opposites. There are sincere, honest, friendly, caring, people online. Learn to discover and know the difference.

People Are Not Always What They Seem

It's far easier to create a persona in cyberspace than IRL. There are no visual or aural clues—clues we normally rely on in our lives to help us come to conclusions about people. For example:

- A 350-pound, bald, 47-year-old man can be a young 160-pound body builder with a full head of hair.

- An overweight, unattractive wallflower can be a svelte life of the party.

You may run into more serious forms of misrepresentation, like these:

- A 14-year-old girl can become a movie star of 30.
- A 16-year-old boy can become the 35-year-old president of a high-tech software company.

When it comes to appearance, there is no way to know whether someone's description is accurate. Of course, part of the fun of being online is the possibility of reinventing ourselves or our life. However, keep in mind that misrepresenting yourself could end in an uncomfortable situation if you decide you want to meet your partner in person.

It is usually difficult for a child to impersonate an adult for very long, or for a person to maintain a successful gender switch online, especially if you talk with these people carefully and learn to be sensitive to the inadvertent clues. Even so, it pays to be extremely cautious. Take the time to ensure that your cyber interest is both an adult and the gender you're interested in.

Vive La Difference?

Some men and women online are looking for the same thing: uncomplicated, uninvolved, impersonal sexual experience. But as a rule, there *is* a difference between how men and women deal with intimacy. In my experience, women prefer some emotional contact, sometimes significant, before they engage in sexual activity—even in cyberspace. Of course, there's always the exception to any rule.

Talk on the Phone and Exchange Photos

Always talk with someone on the phone and request a photo exchange before you plan to meet in person. How many of you have had *truly* successful blind dates? Keep the following in mind as you plan to meet in person:

- If, after talking to someone on the phone and exchanging photos, you're not really sure you should go through with a meeting, don't. You can always reschedule if you change your mind later.
- In all fairness, if you don't find the other person physically attractive, stop the interaction right away. Just as in real life, it's easier to reject someone earlier in a relationship than later.
- If the person you're planning to meet resists sending you a photo, it's a good idea to ask why.

Some people consider their chances of rejection to be lower if they haven't sent a photo, especially if they feel themselves to be unattractive. But the situation will be far more uncomfortable if the person they meet doesn't consider them attractive.

Always Leave Yourself an Out

Never, ever, agree to meet someone without leaving yourself options. Suppose you would rather not be with, let alone have sex with, the person you're meeting? Plan for the following, without exception:

- Another place to stay for the night (research local hotels, for example).
- Transportation to where you are staying and back home again (an alternative, if you were depending on transportation from the person you're meeting).
- A way to bow out gracefully—an excuse, in other words—if you discover you're not interested.

It's unlikely that the person you're meeting is an ax murderer or has a deep-seated psychotic flaw; one unscientific study shows that there are no more wackos online than in the general population. But suppose the photo of your cybersex partner (and possibly IRL partner) turns out to be a dozen years old, and the person's put on 200 pounds in the meantime? Suppose the person's like Pigpen from "Peanuts" and you're particular about hygiene?

Don't Expect to Find Your Life Partner Through Cybersex

It can—and has—happened. But don't plan on it or expect everyone you meet in the adult areas to be a potential mate. After all, the connection came about through cybersex and that tends to make sex the major focus of the relationship. Just as your chances of meeting your future wife or husband through a one-night stand are a little iffy, so are the chances of meeting a life mate when you meet and have cybersex with someone online. There is a difference online, in that the sheer number of people to choose from makes the pace a bit faster than meeting people in the physical world. But be realistic, and you'll enjoy yourself far more.

Be Honest and Ethical

It will be much easier for everyone if you're honest right from the start in your online relationships. Many people I've spoken with feel the following points are key:

- Don't try to be someone you're not.
- Don't omit essential details that could surprise or disappoint—keeping rules of safety and privacy in mind, of course.
- Follow the old golden rule: Tell your online friends the same type of things you'd like to discover about them. If they hedge, you should pause also: something's not right.

The Disadvantages Are the Advantages

Although the relative anonymity of online communication makes it possible for people to be deceitful, it also allows us to express ourselves in ways, both sexually and otherwise, that we might find difficult or uncomfortable in our daily lives. It becomes easier to say what you think and to express what you feel, and that phenomenon "telescopes" time. What I mean by that is, you may find yourself saying intimate things to people you've just met online—the type of thing that you might find difficult to say to people you'd known for years—maybe even to your real-life lovers. One woman who'd been a battered wife said she didn't have to worry that the person she was talking to online would reach out and hit her if that person got angry about what she said.

One place that the casual cybersurfer likes to go for fun and games is the now infamous "hot tub" rooms on some of the national online services. As a hard-working reporter, I joined the party one night. Everyone was very friendly and welcomed me warmly—well, up to a point.

> **PHYLLIS:** Hi, any room in the tub for another lady?
> **JSWA:** Welcome, Phyllis!!
> **GEMINI:** Welcome welcome, here I'll make room for u.
> **FELLOW:** Come on in.
> **JSWA:** How are you tonight?
> **WILL:** Hi, Phyllis.
> **FELLOW:** Water's great.
> **PETER:** Phyllis...come sit next to me.
> **PHYLLIS:** Thanks...is it swimsuit optional, Peter?

I was told that no one was to have on anything above the waist—did I mind this "topless" rule? I didn't, I said, because being relatively flat-chested, I was used to being topless! From that moment on, *no one* said another word to me! Sometimes cyberspace is a lot like the real world after all.

The following is from a series of articles I wrote for *Boardwatch Magazine* on the subject of cybersex.

"About a year ago, I was working as a volunteer on a national online service that had "live chat." And after visiting the open chat areas and receiving several propositions to have "computer sex," I realized that here was a phenomenon that had yet to be explored from inside.

To begin, I went to the anonymous "adult" area and I started asking a few questions like, "What goes on here?" and "Why are you here, what do you want?" In the process, I got to know a fellow I'll call Clark.

Clark was a married man who had a nice family and was happy with his sex life, except for one thing. He really wanted to be tied up and abused by a dominatrix and his wife refused to do this. So Clark would go online, late at night, and with the help of a willing partner, would become someone's sex slave via the computer. Can what he was doing be considered cheating on his wife? Clark's behavior bordered on obsession, and he was pretty indiscriminate about his cybersex partners.

In the next few months, I met other people, but no one was as interesting as a fellow I'll call Randy, who I met quite by accident in a public chat area, with all IDs displayed for all the world to see. (While my ID was not hidden, it was hard to know who I really was, since the ID was customized to identify the forum where I was an assistant sysop.) I recognized Randy's ID right away from another forum. Suddenly, he's talking to me about how old am I, and out of the blue, asks me if I've ever had computer sex. Here's how part of our first conversation went:

RANDY: You've never done cybersex?
PHYLLIS: Cybersex, hmmmm. I don't think that's for me but I can't help but be curious as to what you mean. I've passed a few interesting notes in my time.
RANDY: Hmmmmmmmmm....Difference is doing it live to me, it's making love, only electronically.
PHYLLIS: Wow. You must be single.
RANDY: No, I'm not single, actually. And I'm even a little older than you are. But I have to get to know the person I'm going to be with.
PHYLLIS: Does your wife have a problem with your cyberlovers?
RANDY: Actually, my wife doesn't know about my cyberlovers. She's usually asleep. I guess if she had more time and energy for me, I wouldn't be here.
PHYLLIS: Sorry you're not getting what you need, though this is probably a safe place.
RANDY: Yes, it's safe. Although I have gotten "involved" with a few women. I guess I can't treat it as casually as I thought I might.

My husband and I talked it over, and we agreed that I would go "undercover" and really see what this was all about. My husband would be apprised of what was going on, and he'd be on hand for advice.

During the next week, I'd pop into the public chat area and see if Randy was there, and if he'd "beep" me again. He did, and off we went! Now I had his attention and I was starting to have some fun. And for a couple of months we talked about everything and got to know each other. He sent me email almost every day, and sounded much like the ardent suitor, saying how he missed me when he was out of town and not online. He spoke quite graphically about how much he enjoyed our online "dates." I began to feel like the "other" woman.

But what about Randy's wife? I could understand someone needing "a little extra" (like Clark), but Randy was making a lifestyle out of it. I don't see how his marriage could stay healthy with him making love to his computer screen, sometimes for over six hours at once, while his wife was either asleep or busy doing something else around the house. I wondered, does she know? And how would she feel if she caught him? Didn't she wonder what he was doing in there all the time? Maybe she didn't make love to him as often as he needed, but his obsession had to be detrimental to their marriage.

On a typical night in the two months of our relationship, Randy would go into my forum, where I worked online, and page me into a conference room. We'd get into a conversation, or we'd write a story of sorts, with each of us supposedly playing out the parts. He'd say how much he loved talking to me about anything, and how it didn't have to be sex. He also said how much time he was spending with me, and that he didn't have time for anyone else, and he didn't seem to care. But apparently, that wasn't so after about six weeks. I began to notice that Randy was beginning to act a little different.

Randy broke up with me shortly after that on a Saturday morning. He said he was sorry, but he wasn't getting enough sex from me, and needed more lovers. He'd tried to be "faithful" but just couldn't do it. And after months of courting and hours of lusty chat online, it was over.

Now, as a married woman who spent several months in this "romance," I have an opinion about whether or not this was truly an affair. My conclusion is that it rendered the same psychological effects. I knew going into this what I was after, and my husband stayed apprised, but there was a line of privacy that I had to maintain, and it felt like I was actually having an affair. In fact, there were letters that Randy and I exchanged that I am actually too embarrassed to show to my husband! And now that my "relationship" with Randy is over, I am relieved, but I also have a sense of loss.

Eventually, I told both Clark and Randy that they were the subjects of a study I was doing on married men and computer sex. Randy was very upset and felt that I'd used him; he wondered why I hadn't simply asked him whether he thought it was infidelity or not. So I did.

> **RANDY:** "Traditionally, of course, infidelity is having sexual relations with someone other than your spouse. But, the lines become more blurred here, don't they? For me, in order for cybersex to work, there must be more. There must be some connection, some feeling there. In fact, for me it's what makes cybersex different, and more exciting and enjoyable than erotic magazines.
> **PHYLLIS:** Where does that "enjoyment" and excitement go beyond what might be considered "okay" for a married man?
> **RANDY:** If I had to try to define it, I guess it would be several things. For one, it can be defined in terms of desire: does it make one's desire for one's spouse different? Does one desire one's spouse less? For another thing, it can be defined in terms of time: is one taking time to be online in cybersexual relations that could be used being with one's spouse instead. If one is stealing time, then in a sense it IS cheating, isn't it?
> **PHYLLIS:** So, what you do with your cyberlovers isn't infidelity?
> **RANDY:** Right. To me it isn't infidelity. Period.
> **PHYLLIS:** What do you think your wife would say if she found out about the lovers online? Would she feel betrayed?
> **RANDY:** I don't know what my wife would say, exactly but I don't think I've "betrayed" her in any sense.

When I told Clark that I had been carrying on with him "undercover," and as two separate personalities, he thought it was funny, and was impressed, actually! And he agreed to also share his thoughts on cybersex, and its relationship to infidelity.

> **PHYLLIS**: "As a programmer and a very computer-oriented person, would you say that your "adult" escapades, were, for you, not much different than reading an erotic magazine?
> **CLARK:** Not much different. However, having that live interaction was much more real and arousing. After all, you had not only your own imagination to run wild, but there was someone else to bounce those thoughts and ideas off of.
> **PHYLLIS**: Some folks actually have their solo sex together while online; do you engage in cybersex or computersex?
> **CLARK**: Yes, I "actively" participate. I "interact" as I go along in the conversation.
> **PHYLLIS**: Why do you go online for sexual stimulation in the first place?
> **CLARK**: It's an outlet for stuff that I don't have the nerve to do in person. I would ask my wife to participate in some of my fantasies, but she's very conservative. Also, online, rejection isn't a big deal, you know there is someone else waiting and it's not really personal, not to me anyway.
> **PHYLLIS**: When is sex online too much, in your opinion?
> **CLARK**: When what should be casual becomes an addiction, then you have to have more of it; then you want to have phone sex and then meet and have sex for real. And then, other things begin to slide. For me, sexual stimulation online is fun every once in a while, but hardly an integral part of my life.
> **PHYLLIS**: What do you think would happen if your wife found out?

CLARK: Wow, that's a tough one to answer. The interaction would hurt her feelings, she would think that I found *it* more attractive than *she* is. But that's not true, I find her very attractive, and we have a great sex life. But sometimes, even after making love all night, I'll go online for more. Sometimes I can't seem to get enough.
PHYLLIS: Have you ever gotten attached to anyone online?
CLARK: Just you. <Laughter.>
PHYLLIS: Would you call your online activities adulterous?
CLARK: Why no, because I am not in the category where I would be addicted to it and need it as a narcotic. However, it is very, very borderline and anyone who denies that fact is just flat out lying."

And the debate rages on."

All sorts of men and women, single or married, straight and gay, are engaging in cybersex. Some just want an uncomplicated and arousing experience, while others are looking for love and romance. Most people discover that cybersex is different from what they expected. Cybersex is something you have to do in order to really understand what it is and why it's important to play it safe in the most unusual world of cyberspace. As in real life, when people connect sexually, sometimes something deeper can evolve.

CHAPTER FOUR
▶
Bulletin Boards

WHAT IS AN ELECTRONIC BULLETIN BOARD?

It used to be that "bulletin board" meant the standard piece of wood and cork with push pins holding up important bits of paper. In public places such as supermarkets, bulletin boards have business cards, notices of items for sale, and services. When I refer to a bulletin board here, I mean much the same sort of thing—the big difference is that the computer screen has become the cork and pin, and the public posts (messages) replace the slips of paper and business cards. In the supermarket, only people who shop at that store will see the board, and only a small percentage of those will actually read the messages. When you log on to a local bulletin board on the computer, not only the whole town but *anyone* who might dial in—from anywhere—can see what has been posted.

Local bulletin boards are the most inexpensive way to get online because many of them are free; unless a BBS is national or has an Internet or Fidonet (or other network) link, there is usually no charge. The system operator (sysop) acts as the host for what might be thought of as a computer cocktail party. The BBSs with Fidonet connections shut down in the middle of the night and automatically ship mail among themselves. Some of the sysops pay long distance charges to pick up message echoes from out of town. In many cities, mail comes into several central boards and is redistributed locally from there. The result for the user is national connections, usually for little or no fee.

Local BBSs outnumber the national services by a huge margin—cities like New York and Los Angeles have thousands, but many small towns have more than one. Some of the national BBSs are going the way of national online services by providing local access numbers in the large cities. What has happened as a result is that some of the national bulletin boards have become separate BBSs in each city, each with its own local base of users, and the boards stay in touch through their network link. On a national service, everyone accesses the same database, through local numbers linked together by phone lines.

Obviously, if you've been talking to someone interesting on a local BBS, it's much easier to meet with that person face-to-face than to meet someone on a national board who lives halfway across the country. And with the proliferation of "900" numbers for phone sex—perhaps due to the current search for safe sex—adult BBSs are springing up locally and nationally. But be careful if you meet on an adult board; the fact that the person lives nearby is precisely the reason you should not reveal too much about yourself at first.

CAN YOU GET INTO THIS BAR? DO YOU WANT TO?

Expect to be "carded" every time you try to access an adult BBS or the adult area of a BBS until you prove that you are over 18. When you log onto a BBS for the first time, adult or otherwise, you will be asked a lot of personal information like your name, address, phone number, and age. If you want to access adult (sexually explicit) areas, the sysop will usually ask for a copy of your driver's license, but your license will have your home address on it. If that bothers you, you can also send a copy of a military ID or birth certificate. In Chapter Three, I showed you an example of an application that some sysops require from members interested in gaining access to those sexually graphic areas on their BBS.

Before you sign on, you can try to find out something about the sysop of a board you're interested in since the sysop will have a lot of personal information about you. Call some of the places that have lists of BBSs (mentioned in the following section). Even if a computer store, for example, doesn't have a list of bulletin boards, it may know a sysop because he or she comes by for equipment, supplies, or software. Do a little creative snooping on your own. Look the sysop's number up in the phone book and give a call, if you want to. Why not? Sysops expect to be in touch with a lot of people—they run a bulletin board, after all—and they'd like to have concerned, thinking members on their BBS. They can also be a great help in navigating the board, which can sometimes be very confusing.

IF YOU WANT TO JOIN...

How do you decide what bulletin board is for you? First, survey a list of your local BBSs, which you can get from the following sources:

- most computer stores, and some computer repair shops
- larger software outlets
- a local computer organization, such as BCS (Boston Computer Society) or BMUG (Berkeley Macintosh User Group)
- the back of a local computer newspaper
- the local newspaper's recreation or lifestyles section
- the local college's computer science department
- your nerdy next door neighbor who probably has it committed to memory

On *that* list of local BBSs (if you live in a larger town or city) you'll likely find bulletin boards that cover at least one of the following areas of interest:

- adult (usually sexually explicit)
- Christian or other religious theme
- sci-fi, possibly Star Trek
- games for downloading or playing online
- writers
- alternative lifestyles (gay, lesbian)

- local college or university
- business, sometimes with links to the stock exchange
- political discussions and news releases
- ham radio operators
- seniors, with messaging and news information
- PC user groups
- Mac user groups
- Amiga users
- BBS just there because someone wanted to run one

These lists of local bulletin boards are usually comprehensive and include the BBS name, phone access number, theme, cost (if anything), and the sysop's name. Look the list over carefully and mark those that sound interesting to you. Some BBSs that charge a fee (usually called a subscription fee) are often a good deal for the services they may provide—lots of potentially interesting files to download, Fidonet or Internet connections, or live chat. If you'd rather not spend any money, there usually are a few free BBSs to choose from. Some of the subscription boards allow a certain amount of free time each day; for example, one board allows you 40 minutes of free online time each day, after which there is a fee. Fees can range from $30 a year for unlimited use to a few dollars an hour.

When You're Ready to Sign On

When you sign on to a particular bulletin board, there will be screens with information about fees and the services and files available on the BBS. (See Figures 4-1 and 4-2 for examples of several such screens.) Almost without exception, each BBS is menu-driven, and the menus will outline options such as:

- cost, if any
- requests for donations
- why the board exists

- special areas of interest
- member bios
- who logged on today
- the rules!
- information on the sysops and how to contact them

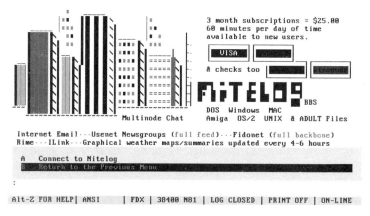

Figure 4-1. *You can see costs and terms of usage, accepted methods of payment, available files, and other information on this screen for the Nitelog BBS.*

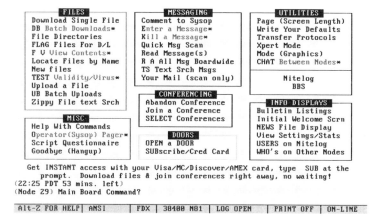

Figure 4-2. *You move around on BBS via various commands; here is a summary of commands for the Nitelog BBS.*

How About That Bio

After your personal information has been requested, the sysop will usually want to know what brings you to that particular board; often, your response is made public. This is so other people using the board can see who else logs on and who has similar interests. Sometimes people are just nosy. If you are asked questions about what you're doing there, or if someone requests a bio, give some thought to what you say, because your response will become your calling card. Assuming you're there to meet people, you could write something like:

"My name is _____(first name only) and I am currently employed as a_____. I'm a graduate of the local college but still like going to night classes to pick up a few new ideas. I've logged onto this board because I'd like to meet some new and interesting people. My interests are_____. I especially like (whatever kind of music you prefer). If you'd like to chat about this or something else, please don't hesitate to write. I am (your age) and single. I have an occasional drink but I don't smoke."

The observant reader will notice I broke at least two of the suggested safety rules: stating your occupation and marital status. But since you're there to meet single people with similar interests, you'll probably want to say enough about yourself to attract others and give them an idea of what you're looking for. Take a minute and think up-front what essential personal details to reveal about yourself, based, obviously, on your own comfort level with issues of safety and privacy protection.

You'll note that I didn't suggest including "please write me—I am single and lonely." Instead I tried, with a straightforward tone, to make this person sound friendly and interesting. Keep in mind that if you say you like the music of AC/DC, you can expect to hear from AC/DC fans—not fans of the Supremes. If you can avoid it, try not to narrow your focus of interests at first. On the other hand, if you truly dislike hard rock music, cigarette smoking, drinking, or something else, you may want to make that known, too. Some people do say things such as "no smokers, please" in their bios. In other words, make a general statement about what you like, and if need be, a definite statement about what you don't. Some BBSs provide more space for your bio than others; this is true on the national services, too. Live chat bios tend to be only a few sentences, while your member list bio can be a whole page, or more. Long bios really aren't necessary. Bios are just a way to give another BBS user an idea of who you are and what you like in order to spark some interest. My sample bio might look like this:

"Hi, I'm Phyllis, a graduate of the University of North Carolina and am a private pilot. I enjoy corresponding with people online and like to hear about their adventures. I work as a writer, and if you're really, really lucky (translation: not careful) you might show up in an article or book that I am writing. I collect teddy bears but lately I've been making them because the kind of teddy bears I like are way too expensive. I also knit and do a little tatting. I like most sports, but especially baseball, like to dance, and am a fan of the ESPN Fitness Pros. And NO MSG, please!"

Whenever possible, use only a first name or an alias for more anonymity. Some BBSs require that everyone use real names only, and then an alias is not an option: but when it is, an alias gives you more freedom of expression.

Help for Newbies

Some boards have a section for new users, which you'll be able to determine from the menu. This is a good place for you to begin. It's not always posted that a person is new to a board but often, if *you* post a message saying you're new, or after your bio goes up on the board, you'll hear from people welcoming you to the board. There will also be how-to instructions either in a section for newbies or in an area that describes the board in general. This will include directions for contacting the sysop (who is there to help) and you should feel free to ask any necessary questions. On many BBSs there is a standard query just before you sign off about whether you'd like to write to the sysop. I found this to be a handy thing when I was new to the BBSs, because by the time I was signing off a board for the first time I was pretty confused. It was nice to be able to post a "help me" message. Most times, these messages to the sysop are sent as private mail.

Don't Forget: Big Brother Could Be Watching

Keep in mind that the sysop can and sometimes must read private mail to be sure there are no drug dealers (or anyone conducting any illegal activities) frequenting the BBS. It's not that sysops are violating your privacy; they're adhering to the law in some states and protecting themselves from liability should something illegal be taking place on the BBS.

Sysops generally read most of what is posted on their public boards to keep the threads organized and to quench any potential or actual flame wars. The fact that sysops must read private mail at times is certainly something to consider when using a BBS for romance or cybersex.

Who Is There—and What Should I Say to Them?

The small, free BBSs usually have only one line, which means when you're online, you're the only one actually using the board at that time. Whatever you type as a public message or greeting can be read by whomever shows up later, same as multi-line, large BBSs and the national services. The subscription boards often are multiple-line, which means that more than one person can be online at once. Sometimes you'll have access to a "Who Is Online" command, which will give you a list of the other people online at that time. Then, if you'd like to talk to someone who is online at the same time you are, you can page them. Many of the multiple line boards have public and private areas for live chat, but expect to pay for them.

First, Sit on the Porch and Watch the World Go By

As you start out exploring the world online, don't feel obligated to jump in and start answering messages right away. I suggest you log on to all the boards that interest you. After cruising the boards for a few days, decide which ones you like best and log on to just those, for starters. If you try to post messages on all the boards right away, you may find yourself confused about what you said where, and you may forget to log back on to some of those boards. Because it can be difficult to remove something once you posted it, make sure you've read far enough through a particular board's messages to know for certain you're truly interested.

Don't expect immediate results from your messages and don't give up too easily. Sometimes regulars don't reply to the first message by a newbie—it might take two or three posts to really get any attention. Try to avoid posting something either publicly or in email that draws attention to the fact that you've gotten no responses. A pitiful "why isn't anyone writing to me" message doesn't make a very positive impression.

Generally, traffic flow on a BBS is fairly constant, but you'll find communication a little slower during holiday weekends. If you pay attention to the times at which messages are posted, you'll learn who is a night owl and who likes to get up early. Some people don't post at all on weekends, and others post only on the weekend. The beauty of BBSing is you can join the party any time you want, no matter how you're dressed or what you look like.

Email on BBSs

Sometimes you may want to respond to a public message with a private email reply. Perhaps your question is a bit off the **thread** (a grouping or connected trail of messages on a specific topic); generally, it's considered good form to stay on topic or start a new thread. You may want to ask the person who posted the public message a question that, for whatever reason, you don't want everyone to see. Or maybe you prefer to get your feet wet by sending an email to someone instead of sending a public message. If you have something especially personal to say to your intended recipient, it's usually best left to email.

The Locals Get Together for a Face-To-Face

Some local boards have "get-togethers" (you'll often see this abbreviated as GTs) at which you can meet some of the regulars in person. These are lots of fun and can be very interesting. However, if it's a get-together of an adult board, be cautious. Many people there will be expecting some sort of sexual activity in good ol' f2f. But if it's a BBS for writers, or Star Trek, or something of a similar sort, I recommend these get-togethers when you feel ready to meet your online friends in the flesh.

Some have weekly or monthly lunches and some just meet on the 4th of July. Afterwards, when you're back online, you'll feel you know who you're talking to a bit better. A group BBS get-together gives you a margin of safety markedly different than meeting that one person you've been writing to; local BBSs have the pleasant feel of a community group.

Mage and I met online back in November of '92 when I began posting in an echo—an area of a BBS where people with like interests can talk about a set subject—known as "Twitland." Twitland's a place "where the bad BBSers go" if you've broken the rules of the board and get **twitfiled** *(means you have your user level access dropped to almost virtually nothing and have only a small amount of access unlike normal users)— or just a place to voluntarily go just to slam insults on the other posters. Of course something like this seems a little intimidating to the more passive folk, but just bear in mind that this particular message echo should never be taken seriously in either your posts or anyone else's.*

Anyway, Mage and I hammered on each other really hard. I was going by my "twit" alias, so he had really no idea it was me when we began talking on a casual, consecutive level, and I didn't tell him until we finally met in person many months later. Although I was "talking to" Mage in Twitland, I wanted to see if there was a more serious side to his flaming nature. So with the handle everyone knows me by, I began talking to him and his brother!

Our messages back and forth to each other started in the usual get-to-know-you type thing, then it evolved into something more personal. Eventually, I gave him my number (at whose request I forget). Needless to say, I was rather nervous when he eventually did call, mostly because he had no idea that the person he was intensely engaging in insult wars in Twitland was me! After

the initial phone call we spent many intimate hours talking to each other. His voice was very mellow, calm, and always reassuring. When we finally met (along with my ex-boyfriend, my mother, his brother and family, as well as a couple of friends of mine from the BBS), I have to say I felt rather awkward. I was very shy towards him in person and barely spoke. Eventually, when I worked up the courage one day to tell him how I felt, I was indeed shocked when he confided his mutual feelings towards me! Now, it's been over a year since we've been together—we've been blessed with a new life, which should have made its appearance in the world by the time this book is published.
—Nightwing, A Longtime BBSer

Typing Conventions

Because we use our faces to express our feelings, and because our faces can't be seen online, there are certain typing conventions and a full range of **smileys** or emoticons, which are meant to be read sideways, that add some mood, nuance, and flavor to the narrative. There are also many abbreviations commonly used in order to save typing time. The following list of conventions and their typical uses is by no means complete or final—people add to it every day!

Convention	Typical use
:-) Smile	:-) How was your day?
:) Smug smile	:) I told you so
;–) Wink	;–) Hmmm, you say you want what?!
;-} Tongue-in-cheek grin	I have no faults ;-}
:=o Surprise	He did what? :=o
:=O Big surprise	He did it where?! :=O

:-(Sadness   My goldfish died :–(
:-{ Frown   You gotta be kidding :-{
;:={ Annoyed   My mute button broke ;:={
:–P Tongue stuck out   Bronx cheer to you buddy! :–P

Feel free to expand on this and make up some of your own. For example, someone with short hair that stands up straight could be =:–), and curly hair could be @:–). Those same people with round faces would be =:) and @:) Let's see, there's also :–] for a wide smile or :–/ for confusion or frustration. Well, the list goes on and on, as you can imagine.

Following are some abbreviations you see in place of the full phrase in the text of messages. Like smileys, the list of online abbreviations is constantly growing.

Abbreviation	Meaning
BRB	Be right back
BTW	By the way
IMO	In my opinion
IMHO	In my humble opinion
IMNSHO	In my not so humble opinion
ROTFL	Rolling on the floor laughing
ISTM	It seems to me
IOW	In other words
SNAG	Sensitive NewAge Guy
YMMV	Your mileage may vary
OBSEX	Obligatory sexual comment
LJBF	Let's just be friends
SO	Significant other

Online, using all caps is considered SHOUTING, so use them only when you'd raise your voice ordinarily. Some newcomers to online communications don't realize this and have to be asked to "stop shouting." Asterisks or plus signs on either side of a word will give it *more* inflection +without+ shouting. Other people use _this_ for emphasis. To convey an action, colons or asterisks ::wiping brow:: are usually *groan* used, too <<wringing hands>>. If it works for you, give it a try!

THE TOUR BEGINS

My first BBS experience was about four years ago when I went online to Thom Foulk's board *Cache la Byte Hub*, a message board that deals primarily with local issues and computing in general. Thom is well known nationally both for his long and lively career in the computer industry, which includes hosting an award-winning national radio talk show, "Computing Success," and his writing for several computer publications, including *PC World* and *Boardwatch Magazine*. He's operated a BBS since 1983, and his board is where he and his friends (myself included) like to hang out. Most of us are so busy and have such varied schedules that without this BBS, we would surely lose touch.

Recently, I logged onto Thom's board because I know him to be very knowledgeable about BBSing. I asked him a few questions about bulletin boards and his opinion on their role in computer communications. Here are a few excerpts of our online conversation:

> From: THOM
> To: PHYLLIS
> My BBS has only about 50 relatively active users. Through our exchange of messages, we have become an extension of a nuclear

family—linked via frequent online discussions, diatribes, debates, and repartee. We know each other. Sometimes, that knowledge feels to be deeper and more intense than if we were office workers sharing a common corridor, or neighbors yelling "Hi!" across the fence.

There is a great democracy and an online commonwealth on BBSs devoted foremost to messaging. No one's got red or black hair; no one's fat, has bad breath, or limps; and it doesn't matter if you're African-American, Hispanic, or any other flavor of minority—or if you're gay, straight, or ambidextrous. In fact, you don't even have to be male or female (my son Dana switched his BBS name to Dan because of the sometimes confusing messages he received from people who were unaware that "Dana" is a gender-neutral name).

You are as you present yourself verbally. For example you could see a rip-roaring debate between a 16-year-old black and a 50-ish WASP retired cop—unaware of the other's physical appearance—and both firing full verbal barrels while mutually accepting their right to be intellectually disagreeable. I've seen debates among users so heated that blows would have been thrown had they been in the same room saying the same words. Imagine such conversations occurring over a backyard fence or in a crowded airport terminal—or just in a typical American living room. They don't, won't, can't, and the fact that they DO in fact occur online is in itself sufficient self-satisfaction for this sysop to continue a single-line, local BBS purely as a community service. I remain continuously curious over the inability of some people to deal with the openness of communication on the BBSs. My BBS, as is true for the vast majority, provides for "private" (everyone else is excluded except the sysop) messages. Some users feel able to communicate only via private messages, and sometimes they get uptight if their innocuous private message becomes public.

It's my opinion that everyone has a deep desire to communicate from a safe soapbox. Everyone likes to brag, reminisce, and gather information from a personal (as opposed to academic) level. BBSing provides an avenue unavailable in any other form of communication. The fact that such communication can reach a deep personal level is somewhat of an astounding side-effect of the process—but it is fact. Two or more people can share their deepest thoughts without regard for all the distracting physical aspects of face-to-face communication. It is so easy for a raised eyebrow—or a raised voice—to add unintended content to a face-to-face dialogue. All parents can recall instances of having said more than they should have in the heat of a situation. All lovers can recall times they wish they could have said more, but the words didn't come at the right time. Everyone can recall these "I-should-have-said..." instances when they didn't have time to compose a meaningful answer. BBS communication allows us to avoid the usual foibles of personal conversation.

A Newbie Gets Started Online

At Thom's suggestion, I logged onto another local BBS to talk with John Morris, who has been online since the mid-'80s, mostly as a sysop. He's had five books published and is a computer programmer. I asked him what would he suggest to the newbie who wanted to get a dialogue going on the BBS. John's advice comes from the sysop's point of view—he elaborated on steps the sysop can take to spark conversations among the people logging onto the board. His advice cuts both ways; the new user can use these same tips toward more successful communication on any online medium:

- **Welcome each newcomer** to the board.

- **Ask an open-ended question** that can't be answered with yes, or no, such as "What do you use your computer for primarily?"
- **Read each message carefully in order to ask more specific questions** in response, such as, "Oh, you keep track of your casino chip collection with your computer. Must be a good sized-collection. What sort of chips are your favorite and why?"

John also recommended that every sysop have enough "feel for human contact" to recognize that there is something interesting in every human being, if only we look carefully. One of the best suggestions for the new user, according to John, is to avoid going online and typing only "I'm new, write to me," which doesn't tell readers much about the writer. He recommends that new users "be human" on the BBS, as discussed next.

> From: JOHN
> To: PHYLLIS
> Browse the message base and respond to some of the communication already in front of you. In short, you let yourself be human. No one with a computer and modem should ever be lonely. In fact, I often find myself advising people to pace themselves, because on the free local systems, you have instant access to all sorts of people. My own problem is that I don't have the time and stamina to keep up with all the old chains of conversation that enticed me in the first place.

> To: JOHN
> From: PHYLLIS
> If advising someone who wanted to get involved in local BBSs, what cautions would you recommend?

To: PHYLLIS
From: JOHN
As an old married fool who probably doesn't know what he's talking about, I wonder if thinking in terms of a relationship as one goes out exploring the BBSs isn't putting the cart before the horse. If I were single again, I swear I wouldn't be out looking for "a relationship," but instead I'd simply get back into circulation, enjoy the company of others, and trust that I would come up with contacts that might develop into something more serious.

I suppose I'd advise someone to look out for the same kind of person they need to be cautious about in any context—someone clearly on the prowl or a little too slick, someone desperate and advertising indiscriminately.

But a BBS's strength as a place to meet compatible people really does lie elsewhere—in its open-door policy. There's no admission. Once you have a computer, modem, and phone line, all you need is a little time and a willingness to say hello, to communicate, and to go beyond "Me Tarzan. Are you Jane?" Maybe it's helpful to have the desire to talk about something other than "you and me." And it seems that things go better when you are being yourself. The neat thing about BBSs is that people show quite a bit about themselves and do it in a surprisingly unself-conscious manner, maybe because they're writing about things that interest them.

In mid-1985 I left my job at a hospital to see if I could write a few more books. My position at the hospital had been such that I circulated among all the floors and got to know nearly all of the 600 hospital employees on a first name basis—from the people in administration to the housekeeping staff. In addition, I had a lot of contact with doctors, patients, the patients' families, as well as agencies and businesses outside the hospital. When I quit, I left to hole up in my basement with my computer and word processor, and suddenly, *I* was unplugged. Talk about a case of the bends. I learned pretty quickly how important my online contacts were to me. Those contacts helped replace the large, elaborate, and quite active network that I lost when I left a good-sized organization.

And I found what I was looking for: business contacts, friendships with people of all ages, people I could call for advice, help, a chat, whatever. I don't know if any BBS "community" is quite definable, but it does have neighborhoods, and people from the different neighborhoods do have things in common with one another, and some of the neighborhoods themselves *are* quite tight-knit communities. Not many people have demanded as much as I do from online connections—but they don't have to. Just a little care and a willingness to participate go a long way.

To: JOHN
From: PHYLLIS
I am sure you've noticed that some folks log on, post a few messages, and then disappear. Why do you think this happens? What's the best way to go about finding what you want from your local BBS? And how long did it take you to discover that the BBS was the way to be in touch with folks, and how long did it take to make those contacts "naturally"?

From: JOHN
To: PHYLLIS
I think some people just aren't able to be patient enough. It doesn't make sense to log on, leave a message saying "Date me," and expect instant success.

The "secret," if there is one, to finding what you want from your local BBS, is to browse existing messages and jump into the conversations. If there are no messages, check the user lists (member lists) to make sure that at least a few people are signing on; then leave notes about personal interests (preferably not too far afield of the board's theme) and *be sure* to call back in timely fashion to pick up your mail.

People who prefer not to expend a great deal of time or energy should probably call around to find boards where the message traffic is already lively. It *is* easier to participate than to try to get communication off the ground.

Back to your questions. Why do people log on once and never come back? It probably takes getting some mail—even just a little—to keep people interested. Also, I've had people chide me as sysop for not doing more to welcome newcomers. So why don't I do more? I'd guess because only one out of twenty new callers will check in again and participate. An aggressive campaign on my part might raise that percentage, but I'd still expend a huge effort for little gain. Over the years, I've spent a lot of energy on messages to people who never called back. But there are steps you can take as a new caller to get more out of your experience on the BBS:

- Call several days in a row.
- Read the message traffic carefully.
- Respond to any notes that interest you.
- Browse for the first few days, but then plan to show real interest in order to get real response.

To put it another way, new callers on established boards are a cheap commodity. In the past, so many people have signed on without calling back that nowadays new callers have to show a little interest to get noticed. Sometimes it does take a little nerve to leave the first few messages. Here's a good way to start:

- Ask specific questions about a specific problem.
- Offer specific responses to a specific item in someone else's message.

- Avoid political and religious discussions unless you feel truly eager to get involved.
- Choose instead the neutral or the positive.

EVERYBODY INTO THE POOL

It's time to go online and see what it's like in the trenches. Keep John's comments in mind as you read through some of the conversations that follow, and imagine what you might say to these people.

Lonely Heart BBS

The first board I cruised was "Lonely Heart." (See Figures 4-3 and 4-4.) It's a singles board, though no doubt the occasional married person does check it out. The following occurred over a few days and does not include every message that was there when I logged on.

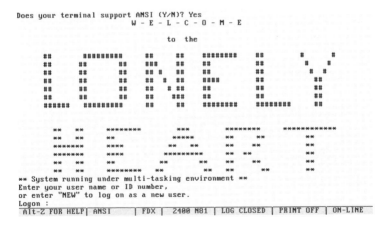

Figure 4-3. *Lonely Heart logon screen*

```
The SysOp is available to chat.
Auto-Message by:           Welcome to the LONELY HEART BBS!
================================================================================
                    MAY YOU FIND A CURE.
         PLEASE TRY TO REFER OTHER USERS TO THIS BOARD.
@@@@@@@@@@@@@@@@@@@@@@@@@@@@@@@@@@@@@@@@@@@@@@@@@@@@@@@@@@@@@@@@@@@@@@@@@@@@@@@@
         PLEASE TRY THE NEW PROGRAMS IN THE DOORS AND GET INVOLVED IN THE GAMES.
              *** THE BIO AND HORROR SCOPE DOORS NOW WORK ***
              *** AND THE MAIL READER IN THE MESSAGES AREA ***
%%%%%%%%%%%%%%%%%%%%%%%%%%%%%%%%%%%%%%%%%%%%%%%%%%%%%%%%%%%%%%%%%%%%%%%%%%%%%%%%
================================================================================
Good afternoon, Mink #30.
You are caller #478,
** PAUSE **
 Alt-Z FOR HELP| ANSI   |  FDX  | 2400 N81 | LOG CLOSED | PRINT OFF | ON-LINE
```

Figure 4-4. *Lonely Heart opening screen*

From: PARTICLE
To: ALL

Hello world, I've made it to the realm of the computer. I've only been around for a short while, so I'm still trying to figure out all of the more exciting "Hot Spots." Anybody have any ideas on ways of filling my unused time?

From: TONY
To: ALL

Hey, all. Thought I'd drop a note to ya. I'm new to this whole computer thing, but it seems like fun. I can be a real conversationalist, so drop me some mail and I promise to respond.

From: NIGHT
To: TONY

Hello, Tony, and welcome to the wonderfully addictive world of BBSing..:}

From: TONY
To: NIGHT

Hi, Night, how are you? I've seen you on a couple other boards. Don't know too many people, so I thought I'd try to get to know you. I don't know too much about computers either—but after a while I thought I was losing touch with what was going on, so I got one. Finally starting to figure this damn thing out. Maybe you could give me some pointers some time?

From: NIGHT
To: TONY

Thank you and it's nice to meet your acquaintance...:} If you need help with your computer, I'll do what I can to talk you through. I'm no computer nerd or anything. Everything I know I've either taught myself or picked up from observation. Also, would I be correct in assuming that you're fairly new to the world of BBSing? I can help you around, considering I've been on these things for 6 years now..:} You'll be amazed at the files you can find and what your system is capable of doing! It's pretty much like having an entertainment system sitting in front of your face..:} I'll explain more about this later if you wish. But I do gotta run tho'. Take good care.

From: VICKI
To: TONY

Hi Tony! Now that you've joined the lavish world of computers....<<grinning>> why don't you tell us a little about yourself and possible interests?? <<curious but quizzical smile>>

From: JOHN
To: VICKI

Hi. I've been in the Air Force for 14 years. I work at the Mountain, for now. I live alone in a house I (and the bank) own. I am very shy and don't like to go to crowded places—a homebody with a daily routine of go to work, eat, sleep, watch a little TV, and do the computer thing. That's about it for my life <<pretty boring!>>. I suppose I'm online to see if someone can spruce it up a bit.

From: VICKI
To: JOHN

Wow! <<amazed look>> Is that your story you're telling? Or mine??<<laughing>> Although, I don't work up on the Mountain. <<wink>>. The shyness seems to go away with the acquisition of a keyboard. Doesn't it??

From: JOHN
To: VICKI

Yes, some shyness goes away when I can communicate with someone one-on-one. Someone with the same lifestyle and objectives as me. It is hard to find someone who fits the bill, even approximately. What about yourself?

From: VICKI
To: JOHN

I find it much easier to sit here and type. People make me nervous and I have a tendency to ramble out of that nervousness. Can you believe that?? <<smile>> As I get older I find that "the perfect" mate is an illusion. I finally decided I needed to learn to stand on my own 2 feet, become a whole person, and maybe, just maybe would have something to offer someone. See?? You asked personal questions, made me nervous and I rambled! Are you happy?? <<blushing....smile>>

   I work in a residential appraisers office. I manage it and am a personal assistant to the owner. They spoil me. Great people to work with and since I'm so far from home, it's the closest thing to family here.

And what do you do up on the mountain?? Oops! IS it classified?? And you are 31?? Ever been married?? Have any hobbies?? Favorite types of movies??

From: SIDEKICK
To: ALL
Just thought I'd drop in and look about, as I fit the profile. Some of you may recognize me from another BBS...well, my name anyway. For those of you who may be interested (and those who aren't), I'm most definitely <<looking around>> <<whispered>> single! For those not quite familiar with my style, you can discount 91.3% of what I say (well, type anyway) as pure misdirection.

For those who care, I'm male, 25, and mostly harmless. Do drink, don't smoke, do program, don't enjoy wearing silly hats, do like baseball (I've missed 3 Sky Sox games this season). I have a technical degree, but refuse to wear a pocket protector.

Finally, I enjoy messaging. I will respond to just about anything (just ask anyone <<Pointing at Vicki>> that I've messaged with). A few of you have met me at get-togethers (some may not remember me too well) and others have not. I'll leave physical appearances to the imagination, unless you can spot me at a ball game.

From: VICKI
To: SIDEKICK
SHEISH! Because I am such a nice person <<coughing behind hand>> and you can put that finger away...it might go off. << nose in the air....very SMUG look>> I will forget the line of your message that stated "I will respond to just about anything" <<big hug>> Nice to see you getting out and about. I knew, I just knew if someone were to ...you might be able to dial a few more boards! <<PROUD SMILE>> Or did someone else dial for you?? <<SWEET INNOCENT SMILE>>

From: SIDEKICK
To: VICKI

Hey, you said yourself that I'll respond to anything. Not exactly those words but the intent was similar ;) Actually, no one really assisted me. I was just making my evening round of crank calls (henceforth to be referred to as my breathing exercises) when I happened upon this one. That high pitched squeal got me so thrilled I even called back :-). In any event, it's nice to see familiar...er...writing styles <<Grin>>.

From: SIDEKICK
To: ALL

Okay, now those of you who have heard this complaint before (esp. from me) stop reading. WHY IS THE RATIO OF MEN/WOMEN 4 TO 1? I realize there are more men (especially in the 18-30 age group) in this area of the country, but I doubt the national ratio is quite that bad. Now, is it because men are (for all you delicate fellas out there, you may want to turn away) more desperate? Is it because men are still more technically oriented in our society and so more likely to use a computer? Maybe someone has other theories? Just a thought. :-0

From: VICKI
To: SIDEKICK

I was just teasing you!! I'm glad to see you here. <<rolling eyes>> I think. <<grinning>> I was also surprised to see that you actually went through the trouble of putting a piece together...um....er....about yourself, I mean....<<wide eyed smile>>

From: MOOSE
To: ALL

O.K. Here goes nothing. I've just finished my first year of college at the University of North Texas and have just now returned home so right now I'm kinda lonely. I'm 18, 6'1" 160lb. endurance runner, studying fire physics, want to fight fires while I'm young and then teach something (I don't know) when I get too old to fight fires. I don't do a whole lot on computers, but most of the people I know think I'm pretty smart (even if I can't spell when I start typing this quickly). My hobbies include working on the car, staying fit, playing a little on the computer, going out to the movies, mountain biking (at least, it was 'til someone stole my bike at college :( ) Drop me a line if you have any questions or would like to know anything more about me.

From: GRAY
To: ALL

Hi everyone.

Thought I may as well stick my nickel in. I am a 36-year-old white male who is very into BBS'ing (messaging and gaming) due to being pretty much homebound. Hobbies are computers and role-playing games and TRADEWARS. Speaking of which, let's play.

From: NIGHT
To: GRAY

Greetings Gray! (Ya sure it's spelled Gray and not Gary? Hehe!) How long have you been into the realm of BBSin? I'm lagging behind on the messaging part, but I do play a few of the online games—not TW2002 tho—so tell us 'bout yourself..:} Have a good one!

From: GRAY
To: NIGHT

Actually it's Gray. As for me; 36-year-old white male with a pot belly (still skinny tho!) pretty much stuck at home for various reasons. Big Tradewars nut <<Looking around with a paranoid manner for Ferrengi Traders.>> also into a bit of messaging and file grabbing...oops! I mean file sharing.<g>

> **From: VICKI**
> **To: GRAY**
>
> Hi Gray! Welcome to the Lonely Hearts. Would it be too forward of me to ask why you're homebound?? <<curious cat smile>>
>
> **From: GRAY**
> **To: VICKI**
>
> Not at all. Just have a bad back and that cuts out 75% of the jobs available in this town. Takes money to do much of anything. Fortunately my utilities are paid for or I wouldn't even run this PC very much. Really been into gaming but just recently deciding to get in on some of the conversations out there. I just started getting back on line after suffering a 2 1/2 month case of PC burnout. When and where is the party going to be?
>
> **From: MOOSE**
> **To: VICKI**
>
> Did someone say party?? Where and when? I'll bring the ice cream.

A chatty group there, yes? Did you notice that some of the folks from the Lonely Hearts BBS really knew how to draw out the others who were less experienced? There were also the "write me, date me" type messages, too, but those messages that really attended to the details of another person got more response.

The MPO BBS

Another board I tried out specialized in astronomy. It was a rather new BBS, and there weren't many folks online yet. (See Figure 4-5.) What follows are chats with a new user, the sysop, and myself. It shows how easy it is to strike up a conversation with almost anyone, even on a new BBS.

```
           WELCOME!
MPO BBS (#70767233)
Running The Major BBS by GALACTICOMM
ONLINE 9600 BAUD AT 12:33 13-JUL-94


The SatisFAXtion board is back!

There is a new library for MPO subscribers only.
Bonus finder charts and ephemerides will be added
each month. The library is MPOSUBS and is visible
only to MPO subscribers.

A viewer for the charts and a few charts are available to
all in the MPOFILES library.

If you already have a User-ID on this
system, type it in and press RETURN.
Your User-ID may be your First and Last
Name (with a space between).

If you are a new user, type "new":

 Alt-Z FOR HELP| ANSI    | FDX  |  9600 N81 | LOG CLOSED | PRINT OFF | ON-LINE
```

Figure 4-5. *MPO Opening Screen*

Forum-Op: SYSOP
Forum Topic: MPO SUBSCRIBER'S FORUM

This forum is aimed at subscribers of the Minor Planet Observer, though everyone is welcome.

The Minor Planet Observer promotes the observation and study of asteroids by amateurs. MPO offers special "Asteroiding Awards" to those confirming the observation of given numbers of asteroids. For more info and a sample copy, leave a message to the sysop.

From: PHYLLIS
To: SYSOP

Hello! I am looking for people to talk to about astronomy. I am hoping to find a public bulletin board for exchange of information and ideas. Please give me a few tips on using this board...thanks! Phyllis

From: SYSOP
To: PHYLLIS

Hi, Phyllis!
Thanks for checking on the board. Getting around is not too difficult—just follow the menus. If you need help at any given menu, type

<ENTER> or "?" and help will follow. The email section is for leaving private notes to others, while the forums are for public messaging. The MPO forum is the primary one for astronomy, though others will eventually come online. There is no restriction to the messages on a forum, though it helps if like topics are kept to the appropriate forum. The files in the libraries are available to everyone for downloading. Uploading requires pre-approval so you can be added to the special group of those who have access to the upload function of this board. Check out the file BBSUSER.DOC in the Main library—it's filled with tips. Hope to hear from you soon and often.

From: PHYLLIS
To: SYSOP

I am interested in talking to others who like to get together as a group and look at the stars and planets. Years ago, while in Nevada, I joined a group of astronomers who met in a very secluded place—with their telescopes—to do some star gazing. It was a wonderful experience and I would like to find such a group here.

From: SYSOP
To: PHYLLIS

I hope to be putting up a 16" telescope before summer's end. At that time, if not before, I plan to have a "star party." I'll make sure you get notice.

From: PHYLLIS
To: SYSOP

I would think that this part of the country is well suited for star gazing...all that open land without city lights. You're getting a new telescope set up? Do tell! How long has this board been up, and what gave you the idea for it? Is astronomy a hobby for you?

From: SYSOP
To: PHYLLIS

I hope to have some more activity once I get some shareware written, offer a couple other things, and put mention of the board in my newsletter.

Something that may be of interest: starting mid-July or August, I'll have finder charts for asteroids online. Those subscribing to the newsletter will get "bonus" charts, while those who do not will get a selection of those in the current month's issue. The images will be screen captures of charts I prepare now for the MPO but compressed into JPEG format to keep transmission time down.

From: BOB
To: SYSOP

Hi Sysop,

As you can see, first time on and just looking around. Received the July MPO today. As to success with 4953 last month, I too only had one chance to see it as I have to travel about 40 miles out to get to dark skies. On June 15, I waited until after 1 a.m. and finally got the area high enough to locate the field stars, but could not see the asteroid. Looking forward to 1620 Geographos next month. Will check back on again in about a week. See you later.

From: SYSOP
To: BOB

Sorry you didn't get to see the asteroid. Joe reported it about 0.8m fainter than predicted. Don't these asteroids have any respect? I, too, am looking forward to Geographos. There should be some good photo ops for several nights.

Ten Forward BBS

Many towns can claim a Star Trek BBS, and mine was no exception. (See Figures 4-6 and 4-7.) The Ten Forward BBS uses a type of software that allows users to quote part or all of the message they're replying to, instead of having to repeat parts of the foregoing message. Quoted material is easily identified by the use of initials and ">" just before the quoted line. Quoting allows users to know exactly what the person posting is replying to, without having to scout around for earlier messages. Not everyone uses quoting—some replies consist only of "yes," "no," or "I agree." Other people will refer back to a foregoing message by including it into the reply. For example: "The reason why your car won't start is because it's got a bad...." as opposed to a response consisting only of "It's got a bad...."

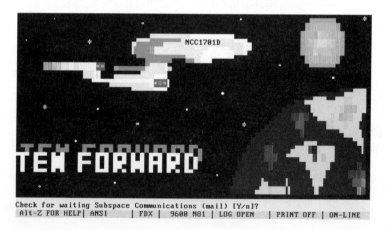

Figure 4-6. *Ten Forward opening screen*

```
Ten Forward: BRIDGE
You must go to the <A>cademy to get registered to use GAMES on this BBS

<N>avagation (how to get around)
<P>rime directive
<M>ain Computer
<S>ickbay
<C>ommunications
<T>ransporter
<H>olodeck
<B>rig
<A>cademy Star Fleat

<G>oodbye      <!>Page the Captain

59 Minutes Left:  Command =>




Alt-Z FOR HELP| ANSI   | FDX | 9600 N81 | LOG OPEN  | PRINT OFF | ON-LINE
```

Figure 4-7. *Ten Forward main menu*

By: PAUL
To: RYAN

RM>Could you tell me any more info on the new series, all I know
RM>is that it is like Star Trek and it is called ST:Voyager!

Frankly that's all any of us know. But rumors are abounding, including that it will feature a ship with new technology which will end up being stolen and taken SO far away from the starting point that it will take the rest of the series to get it home. Rumors about the cast include practically everyone from Lindsay Wagner to Graham Greene. It's scheduled to begin in the third week of January 1995.

By: MATTHEW
To: RITCHIE

=> Quoting Ritchie to All <=-
RF> Did any one catch Patrick Stewart on David Letterman last
RF>night (July 5th)? All they did was talk about soccer and
RF>Shakespeare. No mention of the show or movie. Is he the only
RF>one that does talk shows? I've never seen any of the other

RF> cast members on talk shows.

Yeah, I watched it. Personally, I think it sucked. I didn't watch it to hear about who Patrick felt he was "represented by at the games" or dumb stuff like that. They cut him a little short too. I was hoping for at least a tad about his personal life or something better than soccer.

By: OWEN
To: ROBERT
RW> Gates McFadden did "B" movies and is ashamed of it and is
RW>using her middle name Gates instead of her first name Charlen
RW>or something close to that to prevent the public from
RW>comparing her to those films.

Cheryl Gates McFadden uses her middle name when acting and her first name in her other profession as a choreographer. She choreographed the tap-dancing in the episode Data's Day.

By: OWEN
To: MAUREEN
MG> Does anyone know whether Colm Meany's part on ST:TNG
MG> was supposed to increase? I know he was in the pilot,
MG> with reddish hair and a different name, but then he
MG> became O'Brien. He only had a few lines in the
MG> transporter room for quite a few episodes.

He was meant to be a recurring background character, but eventually became a major recurring character and eventually a regular on DS9. I don't think that it was envisioned that he would become anything more than a backgrounder.

By: JEREMY
To: ALL
I just have one thing to say after watching all those episodes of Star Trek. How can they be SOOOO smart, yet unable to find a cure for going bald? I mean, ya watch the crew of the Enterprise (Next Generation) defeat the overwhelming wonders of the universe, yet they still can't figure out how to give that Picard dude a full head o' hair. From a constantly lost and wondering mind...

It's probably clear to you by now: if you're not a Star Trek fan, you're probably not going to want to spend much time in this BBS, or even log on in the first place. The Ten Forward is a good example of a BBS devoted to a specific topic. Unlike the Lonely Heart board, where people gather just to chat about anything and everything, or even the astronomy board, where there might be information of general interest on star gazing, The Ten Forward BBS wouldn't be such a good place to go if you weren't a Trekkie and up on your Federation trivia. But it was a lot of fun to lurk around on—you can see there is a lot of humor available out there. You never know what you'll find when you cruise the postings on a public BBS.

Heaven's Gate BBS

For a change of pace, I visited a very casual (no specific denomination) Christian BBS and posted a few notes. (See Figures 4-8 and 4-9.)

Here's how it went:

From: PHYLLIS
To: ALL
Hello folks!
 A few of my single friends, tired of the "bar scene," asked me for some advice on meeting people. I am married, but I wrote letters to

my husband before we met in person. I think it's best to get to know someone's mind first and become friends first. I'm wondering if my Christian friends might be able to make some new, possibly special friends here—maybe even spouses. What do ya'll think? Should they get computers and log on? Please answer publicly if you don't mind so we can get everyone involved. Thanks.

From: NORA
To: PHYLLIS

Hello Phyllis,

I think that computers are a great way to meet people and to keep in touch with established friends. I am 20 years old and I have met/talked to some wonderful people through the computers. I also keep in touch with my friends that I made in college. (I just recently moved out here in December.) Welcome them aboard, we love to talk.

```
              )      H E A V E N ' S    G A T E   B B S     (
                    --------------------------------------------
                    Therefore we are buried with him by baptism into death:
                    that like as Christ was raised up from the dead by the
                    glory of the Father, even so we also should walk in
                    newness of life.
                                                              Romans 6:4
Welcome to HEAVEN'S GATE
ANSI detected
                             A Going BBS For A Coming Christ

                    Being then made free from sin, ye became the servants of
                    righteousness.
                                                              Romans 6:18

                    *)*)*)*)*) New Bulletin #5 = Topic Helps (*(*(*(*(*
                    Please take a look at the new Topic Helps in the Bulletin Section
                         Bulletin #5. Topical Bible References & Topic Helps

What is your FIRST name?
Alt-Z FOR HELP| ANSI     | FDX | 9600 N81 | LOG OPEN   | PRINT OFF | ON-LINE
```

Figure 4-8. *Opening screen for Heaven's Gate*

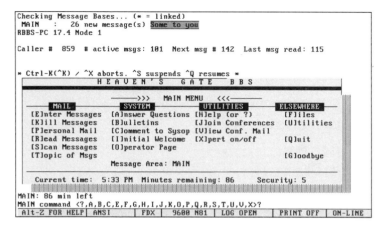

Figure 4-9. *Heaven's Gate main menu*

From: DEAN
To: PHYLLIS

Sounds like you have a good idea, Phyllis! That's an interesting observation that you meet a person's mind first on a BBS! And then meet the rest of the person (bodily) later, perhaps. We had a coffee get-together recently at <a local restaurant> so we could all meet the rest of the people we've been talking to.

From: PHYLLIS
To: DEAN

Dean;
Sure, you do meet a person's mind on a BBS...because there is nothing here but thoughts. You have no idea who I am physically, but here you are reading my thoughts as they go from my head to my fingers, keyboard, computer, modem, and then onto this BBS.

My husband and I are regulars (have been for a while) on another BBS. We already knew the sysop but have since met with the others two or three times. It was fun for both of us.

From: ERIC
To: ALL

Hi, my name is Eric, I am also fairly new to this board. I like music, games, I am very active, and I like computers. I am interested in getting to know some of the people on this board and hopefully many other boards as well...thank you!

From: DEAN
To: ERIC

Hi, Eric. Just wanted to say "Hello" to you and welcome aboard Heaven's Gate BBS!!! Have a good day!

From: ROCK
To: PHYLLIS

Howdy Phyllis!

My name is Rock, and I'm one of the co-sysops on here. I think that you've hit the nail on the head! Christian BBSs are a GREAT place to meet new and wonderful friends. As a matter of fact, if we had enough interest in it, we could create a new conference area on Heaven's Gate just for singles! Right now we have a Youth area that is going strong. Talk to your single friends and ask them what they think about a Singles conference area. If they would like it, I'm sure that we can arrange it. Thanks for your sensitivity to this need. It's great! Oh, and by the way...Welcome!

As you can see, in this BBS there were a few variations on the "hi, write me" notes that the sysops talked about earlier in the chapter—those notes may get you *some* response, but why not think of something a little more original?

DECIDING FOR YOURSELF

Perhaps you got an idea of what folks are like online as you were reading through these messages. Maybe you also have a better sense of the impression you'd like to make (and not to make!) when you get online and start posting messages publicly. As mentioned earlier, some BBSs give you the option of using an alias, but keep in mind that the sysops of local BBSs can look up who you really are, and they also have access to private messages. If you do use an alias you can always tell someone your name later; as I've mentioned before, aliases may give you a little more freedom of expression because you are anonymous to everyone but the sysop.

BULLETIN BOARD SOFTWARE CAN GET CONFUSING

Because several different companies publish software for bulletin board systems, make sure to read through the bulletins on using each new board you sign onto. For example, some boards call the public messaging bases "conferences," while others call them public message areas. The differences between the types of software can be confusing, but once you've logged onto a few bulletin boards, you'll understand better how to navigate, recognize, and understand the commands you find there. If you keep at it by logging on frequently, it will soon become familiar. Also, there are always people online who will be glad to help. Keep in mind that because these boards are local, you can post a private message to the sysop and ask him or her to call you and help you through it.

You do compromise your privacy when you give out your phone number, and you'll be asked your address and phone number the first time you log onto a local board. Think again about getting a P.O. box number or using your work address.

ADVANTAGES OF LOCAL BBSS

Local and national boards serve different purposes, but both will give you the opportunity to meet people for friendship, dates, to aid in the search for mates, or just fool around. The biggest and perhaps only advantage to local boards is they are cheap, plentiful, and that the object of your desire is probably close by. For sheer numbers of people to choose from, it's hard to beat a national online service. Email on the national online services is not monitored and is considered private between the sender and receiver. The only kind of local BBS that comes close to a national service is one with an Internet connection (which will probably cost you something) and those with a network echo, like Fidonet, which does a message swap with all the other boards connected across the country. With some experience you can decide whether you prefer local BBSs to national BBSs, or to commercial services, which we'll profile in the next chapter.

CHAPTER FIVE
▶
The Commercial Online Services

In this chapter I'll take you on a quick tour of the major national online services: America Online (AOL), CompuServe (Cserve or CIS, for CompuServe Information Service) Delphi, GEnie, and Prodigy (P*). I've learned about these services by getting a lot of help from experienced onliners, just as you will. In some ways I am still a novice, and I continue to take advantage of the good online help.

As I review each service, I'll focus on the areas conducive to meeting people. (See Chapter Three for online typing conventions, and for tips on posting public messages and sending email; those tips apply to all the national services.) I'll give my opinion of each service as I go, and I'm sure that some people will disagree with me. I'll give you an overview of places you may want to check out, though there are many others, too. This will be a nontechnical tour for the person who wants to go online to meet and talk to people and get information. For the most part, that is how I've approached my review of these services.

Before getting started, I need to spend a little time reviewing technical terms such as terminal communications programs, access software, offline readers, and front ends—all tools to aid you in your travels online. A **terminal communications program** is a program that tells your modem to dial a number you've given it in order to connect with an online service or BBS. It differs from access software, which is designed for only one service. **Access software** is provided by the service itself as the only means of signing on that service. AOL and Prodigy provide access software. A **front end** is a program that gives the service an interface whose main purpose is to enable the user to navigate more easily. An **offline reader** is a program that gets messages and email that you've requested from the service. It then presents the messages and email offline in a form that you can use both for responding to and generating new mail and messages. Most front ends have offline readers in them. If you're confused, don't worry, you don't have to have the definitions down pat to successfully use the programs.

As online communication proliferates, a large number of people are choosing to subscribe to more than one national online service, and a growing number of people are on several of them. Each service is unique and will bring something different into your life. I hope you'll find this review helpful as you decide where to go first, and then maybe, where you'll go next.

GETTING STARTED WITH PRODIGY

Prodigy's user-friendly access software package is very easy to use and is readily available in most computer software stores. Many new computer systems come with Prodigy already loaded. If you know someone who is online there now, they can also get the software for you. DOS, Macintosh, and Windows software start-up packages are available.

Prodigy was designed to be user-friendly, with lots of pictures and easy-to-access online help. Its graphical user interface lets you click on pictures or graphics that represent what you want to do. You do, however, have to use Prodigy's software to log on and use the service; *you can't use terminal communications programs like you do for local BBSs.* The Prodigy Service software logs on only to Prodigy, and no other communications software can log on to Prodigy. The advantage of this set-up is that you don't have to do anything except type in your ID and password to log on each time; the interface does everything for you. In fact, as long as you know your password and ID, you can log onto your account from any computer anywhere in the country that has the software loaded, a modem connected, and Prodigy's local number.

Who Is on Prodigy?

There are many computer novices on Prodigy, and a lot of their kids (who may know more about computing than their parents!). There are probably more beginners and more first time users on Prodigy than any other service. There are also some fairly high-powered people in the computer industry who use Prodigy. One reason for that is the consistent availability of fresh news about the computer industry—and the opportunity for those computer mavens to be in touch with a lot of beginners. Many computer hardware and software companies are on Prodigy with their own support areas, and they've been there from the start, back in 1988. A low percentage of Macintosh users are on Prodigy, possibly because Mac users have had America Online since 1985. Apparently, many Mac users felt no need to make the switch—particularly since they were happy with American Online (better known as AOL, an online service we'll cover later in this chapter).

When Prodigy went online, it was the first service of its kind for DOS-based PCs (in the majority at the time), and it boasted a graphical, easy-to-use interface. It was easy, inexpensive, and its possibilities seemed endless! It kept many people, previously inexperienced in the online world, entertained for hours, wandering through cyberspace and talking to each other through public messages and swapping email with people all over the country. In the years since Prodigy went online, the number of households with computers has exploded, and there are very few offices without computers. Online users over time have developed different views on what they want in an online service, and many have outgrown Prodigy. But if not for Prodigy, many people would not be online at all.

Email beyond Prodigy

A very helpful piece of software that Prodigy provides for its members is Mail Manager (mentioned at the beginning of this chapter) for offline reading and writing and automatic sending of email. Mail Manager also allows you to easily send and receive mail on the Internet. This Internet connection means that you can send email to anyone on any BBS or national online service that has a link to the Internet. Mail Manager is the only way to get and send Internet mail on Prodigy. Any member can download it.

Navigating

Prodigy has many public bulletin boards of quite varied subject matter. Some of the good areas to meet people include Hobbies, Collecting, Sports, Family and the live chat options. Some of the custom forums have live chat, but there is also a forum just for chatting. (Prodigy's Windows software is required for chat areas, and this software can be downloaded online if you don't have it.) In Prodigy's Chat forum, you can also create a room for just two, three, or however many people you want. You can set up a room with a special password so that only certain people can get access.

If you post a public bulletin or send email, your name and ID will show. However, in Chat, you can choose a nickname that can't be traced. Some people try to sign on to Prodigy with fake names, but it's not allowed; a credit card number with the corresponding name has to be used. It is my understanding that the management of Prodigy wants the service to be a wholesome, educational experience for children and adults. (This is not to say that other services encourage immoral or unethical behavior; they have ways to protect children, too.) On Prodigy the holder of the "A" ID (the primary name given for the household) can lock the other sub-IDs (B–F) out of all but the basic services and can then monitor the sub-IDs' activities.

Finding People Online and Being Found

Prodigy has an easy-to-access member list that is handy for finding people and for being found. Imagine you've been wondering if an old school friend is on Prodigy, but you have no idea where she lives now. All you have to do is search on her name! It's also handy if you want to know more about someone you've been talking to online. If the member has chosen to be listed, the member list will show the ID and the city and state the member was in when she or he first signed on. It can be used for checking who is on a sub-ID under the same last name. For example, if someone says she isn't married, but her "B"-ID is being used by someone who has the same last name in the same location and is of the opposite sex, then you'd better hope that's the name of one of her kids!

Not everyone on Prodigy chooses to be on the member list, and it is up to you to decide if you want to be on it. If you get an unpublished phone number and a P.O. box, you may feel more comfortable making your name and general location public. It's up to you; weigh the risks and the benefits for yourself. When you go into the Prodigy Chat areas, you can also write a short bio about yourself that contains whatever you want to include.

Dating and Mating on Prodigy

Prodigy is an excellent place to meet people. It's full of public messaging forums—you'll find it is difficult to run out of either places to go online or public messages to read. It's like several hundred local BBSs bunched up together, yet available to everyone in the United States.

Once you've met someone you're interested in, you can search for public messages posted to or from him or her in any of the bulletin board areas—perfect for lurking in while you get to know the object of your interest. There is also the live chat option in some forums, which provides a good place to hang out and get to know people as well.

What Is It Going to Cost?

If you use Mail Manager for email, and select the public messages you'd like to read offline using Bulletin Board Manager, plus faithfully monitor the time you spend in live chat, Prodigy can be quite reasonable. There are also several pricing plans available as of 10/12/94. (All amounts are in U.S. dollars and, like everything, are subject to change.) These fees are for the entire household (ID's A–F). The Value Plan is $14.95 for an unlimited amount of time in Core and five hours in Plus areas. Any extra hours spent in Plus will run you $2.95. With the Basic Plan, it's $9.95 for five hours Core and Plus combined, and $2.95 an hour for Core or Plus after that. There is no extra charge for 9600 bps service in all plans for most features.

The Feel and Flavor of Prodigy

In terms of navigation, Prodigy may be one of the easiest of all the national services. The graphical interface not only guides you to where you want to go, it entices you to go other places you might not have considered otherwise. For example, you sign on, and up comes the opening screen. (See Figure 5-1.) You notice a news item: "Tonya's ex gets 2 years in jail" and you say "I wanna hear about that!" So you enter the number 3 and hit Enter, or you click your mouse on number 3, and Prodigy takes you to another screen with all the news on Tonya Harding's ex. Prodigy's headlines are updated constantly, so the latest news is always available to you.

Figure 5-1. *Opening Prodigy Highlights screen*

If for example, you like to travel, you might use "JUMP" to get to Travel Highlights. (See Figure 5-2.) The opening screen for Travel (see Figure 5-3) comes up, and suddenly you're wondering, "How are *my* state's highways doing?!" Next thing you know, you've selected option #2 and you're off.

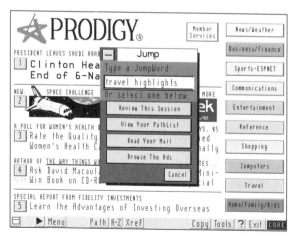

Figure 5-2. *Prodigy JUMP window to travel highlights*

Figure 5-3. *Prodigy's travel highlights screen*

Prodigy is very friendly and, as a result, very forgiving. If you make a mistake, a message box pops up and tells you what's wrong, so you'll know to try something else. However, for some people, Prodigy's screens "paint" (that's when each screen comes into view on your computer) too slowly, and they don't care for the advertisements at the bottom of each page.

If you've never been online before, especially if you're new to DOS-based computing in general, Prodigy is a great place to start. I've been on Prodigy for years, and though I'm no longer a beginner, I still enjoy and use the service quite a bit. It reminds me of taking an elegant, leisurely train ride through the best parts of each city and town on the way.

GETTING STARTED WITH GENIE

While I was on Prodigy I met Harold Day, who told me about GEnie. Harold had been on GEnie for several years and was a big help to me as I learned my way around. GEnie was quite a shock after Prodigy, because it's all ASCII text, by which I mean lines of words scrolling across the screen. (See Figure 5-4.) You don't have to use special software to get online; terminal communications software will work. Most people download the program Aladdin, which makes navigation around GEnie easier. Aladdin lets you upload and download messages and email that you can read later when you are no longer online. At first, I missed the comfort and color of Prodigy, but once I got used to GEnie and started using Aladdin, I really liked what it had to offer.

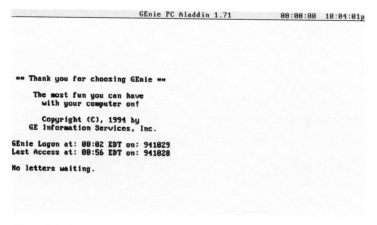

Figure 5-4. *GEnie opening screen*

Who Is on GEnie

I couldn't tell you the standard profile of a GEnie user, even after years of using GEnie myself. From what I can tell there is a good cross-section of all types of people online. There are some of the most knowledgeable people, writers, and movers and shakers in the computer industry online, as well as a healthy helping of newbies, hobbyists, gardeners, and arts and crafts people. But there are people in cyberspace, as in the computer community in general, who aren't comfortable with anything but a graphical user interface like Prodigy or AOL, and those people are unlikely to be comfortable with GEnie, no matter who is on there or what it has to offer.

GEnie Email and Beyond

You can send your email using Aladdin; avoid composing email while you are actually on line because you can't edit as easily, and you'll eat up a lot of valuable online time. As with any service, if you get knocked offline due to a power hit or phone line noise, anything you've written will be lost, unless it was first written offline using a program like Aladdin. GEnie also has a link with the Internet, and you can write to anyone with a link to the Internet through the Internet **gateway** (the connection point between two separate systems).

Navigating

You can access GEnie from one of several terminal communications programs (like Procomm Plus), then navigate manually by typing in commands. I suggest you use Aladdin, or another **front end**, which adds to the flexibility of the service. I don't recommend using GEnie without a front end or offline reader because those programs make uploading and downloading much faster and easier—and as mentioned earlier, it saves time online, which saves you money. There are several offline readers for Mac users, but I've been told (and this is not my opinion—I don't have a Macintosh) that the fastest and most popular is GEnieNav. Using Aladdin made GEnie very easy for me to use, and very fast. If you are a Mac user, plan to visit the Mac-related roundtables on GEnie to find which offline reader is best for you. As a PC user, I feel that Aladdin *is* GEnie; for the most part, when I talk about GEnie, it is from an Aladdin user's point of view. If you have a Mac and plan on using GEnieNav, it won't be much different than using Aladdin.

Where the People Are

Each of GEnie's common interest areas is called a **roundtable** (RT), and within each roundtable are public message areas. (See Figure 5-5 for an example of a roundtable opening screen.) Members can also chat live in a roundtable conference, known as a **real time conference** (RTC). Some RTCs are regularly scheduled, but you and another person can go into that area and hold a conference anytime you like. While in RTCs, you can talk among all the folks in the room as well as send private messages to individuals.

```
                    GEnie PC Aladdin 1.71         00:00:00   1:01:44p
                        File COLLECTI.BTN
- - - - - - - - - - - - - - - - - - - - - - - - - - - - - - - - - -
                Welcome to the Collectables RoundTable
- - - - - - - - - - - - - - - - - - - - - - - - - - - - - - - - - -
          ************************************************
          *       COLLECTABLES ROUNDTABLE RTC SCHEDULES        *
          ************************************************
Conference                                Day         Time        Room
----------                                ---------   ---------   ---------
Garage Sale Junkies................every..Monday.....10PM.EST.......3
Hallmark Collectors...............2nd+4th.Tuesday...10PM.EST.......3
Refunding.........................every..Wednesday..10PM.EST.......3
Sweepstaking......................every..Thursday....9PM.EST.......3
General Collectors................1st+3rd.Thursday..10PM.EST.......2

If you have any questions or concerns please send Feedback COLLECT$

    Esc Exit                    ↑/↓ Move one line         X Extract
    F7 Mark block start      PgUp/PgDn Move one screen    S Search
    F8 Mark block end     Ctrl-PgUp/PgDn Move to top/bottom
```

Figure 5-5. *GEnie Collectables Roundtable welcome screen*

GEnie also has a forum just for chatting. There are several different rooms you can go to and either chat or play interactive games with other members. You can also send private messages or create your own little sub-room where you and another person can talk privately without interruption.

There is also a roundtable only for adult discussions, but you need to apply for permission to access this area. The adult area is part of the Family Roundtable, and there are bulletins telling you where to write for entry to these adults-only discussions. This is GEnie's way of keeping kids out of areas that may contain unsuitable material!

While online you can see who else is on, and from individual RTs, you can search on public postings of other members and find out, by lurking, what some of your potential friends are interested in. RTs are a great place to meet people, and they all have chat options.

Dating and Mating with GEnie

From the main menu you can access the member list manually and see whether anyone you know is online. *You* can be found through the member list, too, in a similar manner to Prodigy. GEnie is also a great place to meet people for whatever fun and games you have in mind. GEnie's chat areas, while challenging to use at first (because there are commands to learn), are flexible enough to allow as intimate a conversation as you could possibly want. For meeting people with interests similar to yours, GEnie's strength is in its roundtables, files, and information.

What's It Going to Cost?

If you do all of your navigating of GEnie offline using Aladdin, GEnieNav, or another offline reader, GEnie is a good value. GEnie has a rate of four hours a month for $8.95 when you log on only between 6 p.m. and 8 a.m. on weekdays, or all hours on the weekends and some holidays; it's $3.00 for each additional hour. Time you use from 8 a.m. to 6 p.m. weekdays is billed at $9.50 an hour. (Note that here, as elsewhere, prices are subject to change.) I often check how much time I have left at the end of the month, and then if there is some extra, I use it up in a live chat or conference with my friends during the 6 p.m. to 8 a.m. time slot.

The Feel and Flavor of GEnie

Once you've learned to use Aladdin or GEnieNav, GEnie is very quick and easy. The average user can access many message bases, send email, and get messages in a matter of minutes per day. GEnie has all the power of any other online service without the frills and pretty graphics. GEnie's Aladdin was the first offline reader I used, and I found my ability to communicate increased because I could take more time to read and write offline. I like the people I've met on GEnie—they seem lively, fresh, and a lot of fun. There is an openness, a free feeling on this service, almost like a large outdoor festival.

GETTING STARTED WITH DELPHI

The next national service I tackled was Delphi. I saw an ad for it, believe it or not, on Prodigy! I used good ol' Procomm Plus (a standard terminal communications program) to log on (though once online, information is available on front-ends and offline readers). Logging on with any terminal communications program is very easy.

Who Is on Delphi

Communication on Delphi tends to be very lively, *and it's sink or swim in terms of your ability to communicate through your keyboard.* That's not to say that the service is difficult to use, just that Delphi members are gregarious and love to chat—expect to have to think on your feet. Delphi can be a crash course in communication.

There is a lot of cybersex on Delphi, also, but it's far from being a cyberspace "sex network"; many of the folks online are interested in more than just hot chatting. They are debating everything! All sorts of discussions pop up at any time with anyone, whether you're in a forum's conference area or the general conference area, or just cruising around—which I actually prefer.

Who are these people on Delphi? I find that they don't follow any particular convention. For example, so many user IDs are androgynous that I can't tell whether there are more men than women or vice versa. Suffice to say there is a very interesting mix online! Hence, the need to be able to clearly transfer your thoughts from your brain to your fingers to your keyboard.

Delphi is very powerful if you know the commands; however, like GEnie, it's a text-based program. Delphi looks very unadorned and basic at first, but you can do everything online there that you can anywhere; though you won't find a graphical user interface like Prodigy, there are help menus everywhere you go.

Email and More

There are several **offline readers** (Rainbow, D-lite) you can use with Delphi, and they are all useful for a quick trip through the forums or your emailbox. For navigating manually and live chat, I use Procomm Plus, which offers a **split screen** (also known as **chat**, or **conference mode**) for live chatting, as do some of the other offline readers and terminal communications programs. (See Figure 5-6.)

Using Delphi

Even with no front end, Delphi is easy to navigate. You only need the first few letters of any command, all listed on every page, to execute that command. (See Figure 5-7 for an illustra-

```
                                   REMOTE
.sey.> Hi Phlegar
.Macronym> no way
.Karn Evil 9> They hate rap and country
.Macronym> no country no rap
No country!
PHLEGAR> No country!
.Garou> hi Phe;
.Garou> 1
.Macronym> no country...you heard it thrice from me
.sey.> I'm listening to country right now:)
.Karn Evil 9> they like harp music..lol
.Garou> BOO!
.Macronym> ahhhhhhhhhhhhh no country
.Garou> welcome to my house o' sppokiness
Harp music? How soothing.
PHLEGAR> Harp music? How soothing.
.sey.> guess so Karn:)
                                   LOCAL
Howdy!
No country!
Harp music? How soothing.

                       Chat Mode - Press ESC to end
```

Figure 5-6. *Procomm's split screen*

```
Welcome to DELPHI
Copyright (c) 1994
Delphi Internet Services


Logon at    : 13-JUL-1994 15:00:36
Last Logon  : 12-JUL-1994 21:35:55




MAIN Menu:

Business and Finance        News, Weather, and Sports
Computing Groups            Reference and Education
Conference                  Shopping
Entertainment and Games     Travel and Leisure
Groups and Clubs            Using DELPHI
Internet Services           Workspace
Mail                        HELP
Member Directory            EXIT

MAIN>What do you want to do?
 Alt-Z FOR HELP| ANSI     | FDX |  2400 N81 | LOG CLOSED | PRINT OFF | ON-LINE
```

Figure 5-7. *Delphi's opening screen*

tion of Delphi's opening screen.) It's an easy-to-use, menudriven system with plenty of help along the way. One of the great things about Delphi is that there is always someone somewhere online who can go into a conference with you to help you out.

Where the Boys and Girls Are

On one of the very first days on Delphi, I met a writer named Ted Remington. (We've stayed in touch via email over the years.) I asked him a lot of questions about Delphi, which he uses almost exclusively.

Ted knows from experience that there are a wide variety of public forums known as **special interest groups** (**SIGs**), ranging in interest from writing to New Age to gay issues to entertainment. Every SIG is available to all members. Then there are the **custom forums**; on Delphi, these allow people with fairly specialized common interests to get together and pay a small fee to use this area privately. Members of these custom forums can make them accessible to new members, who can come in from the public areas of Delphi and post messages just as they would in the SIGs. If the public custom forums generate enough interest and dollars of revenue for Delphi, often Delphi makes them available to all at no extra charge.

There are many custom forums on Delphi not open to anyone except by invitation. These closed forums are useful to members who don't want just anyone coming in and posting notes or lurking. As Ted puts it, in a closed forum you don't have to "put up with the kooks or the flamers." Anyone can start a closed forum by applying for one with Delphi. The forum creator pays a charge to Delphi; no one will know of the custom forum's existence unless a member tells them. The area is listed in the menu as Custom forum XX (XX being the number), with "private" after the number. The common interest of the forum is then not revealed. This would be ideal for, say, a cyberswingers club; perhaps you met some couples in an open forum and decided to get together privately. Or you could create a singles club, and you'd be able to check out each potential member. Yet another idea—a special interest sex club where everyone is into leather or latex. You get the general idea.

Be forewarned that these private areas can hide the disturbing side of life, such as clubs for bigots or potential sex offenders who misrepresent themselves to Delphi and are able to have their private get-togethers unobserved. Parents using Delphi should investigate immediately and thoroughly if their kids mention anything about "a nice person online" giving them passwords into "special areas."

Each SIG or custom forum on Delphi typically has several areas: chat, database, and a forum where people post and respond to open messages. There is also a poll area where people can post polls to be answered by the other users, and an Internet area, which gives you access to the Usenet (all newsgroups with the same themes as the custom forum) part of Internet. For example: A writers group would be interested in seeing information pertaining to writing only.

Delphi has full Internet access for a small fee each month. This includes **Internet Relay Chat** (IRC), which allows you to chat online with any Internet user in the world with access to IRC. For example, Ted has talked to people in Europe, Asia, and Australia just as easily as he and I often chatted. (See Chapter Six for more information on the Internet)

Dating, Mating, or Fooling Around

Once you learn the ropes, Delphi is great for meeting people. But that freedom unfortunately allows for the type of deceit and concealment that I discussed in Chapter Two. Everyone writes a customized online bio, which makes them fun to read, but you have to wonder how much of each bio is true. I guess the attitude on Delphi is "who cares?". Its freedom makes live chat options available to anyone at nearly anytime, and if you talk to someone long enough—and you are careful—you will probably discover what you need to know about that person. From my experience, there are a lot of very interesting and open-minded people on Delphi.

Delphi's Costs

It's no wonder that Delphi has been considered a great place to chat for years—it's very inexpensive: for a one-time sign-on fee of $19 (less, if the 20/20 option is chosen in the first month) you can access Delphi for 20 hours a month for $20, and then $1.80 for each additional hour. That's a lot of inexpensive chatting, and many Delphi's members have two $20/20 accounts. This gives them over an hour per night to chat, and those rates are for 6 p.m. to 7 a.m. weekdays and all hours on the weekends. For that same rate, plus $3 per month, you can also chat live on the Internet, too, as mentioned earlier. If you don't plan on being online that much, you can choose four hours per month for $10, also from 6 p.m. to 7 a.m. weekdays, and all weekend. (Keep in mind, as elsewhere, that these prices are subject to change.)

The Feel and Flavor of Delphi

Delphi has a very distinct feel to me, like going through a series of intriguing tunnels and caves. Wherever you turn, there is something different and interesting going on, and just when you think you've seen it all, someone tells you about a new forum or an ongoing discussion group. The people running Delphi have (in some ways) turned over some of this service to anyone who has the money to open up an area by virtue of the custom forums. Unlike any other service, Delphi's custom forums are very inexpensive and easy to set up. That and the other attributes of Delphi make for a constantly evolving service, with what seems to be a unique group of members. Delphi's text-based (ASCII) system makes it accessible to the blind, as do other text-based online services.

I finally got my modem and software working in December 1993 and joined a now defunct national online service and also became a regular on a local BBS. Well, anyway, I am now on Delphi and corresponding right now with a woman about 1500 miles away. We have never met but I have really grown close to her and her three children. I was a skeptic at first because nothing can replace that good old face-to-face physical contact. She was introduced to me by another friend I met online and we have been writing back and forth ever since.

I can't really say we have a romance going but I would like to meet her and may do so later this summer. I think the real cyberspace equalizer is not only the removal of racial or disability barriers but that when you are alone with your thoughts and the keyboard you are more likely to type out feelings that you might be too inhibited to say face-to-face until you got to know someone better.
—Harvey, on Delphi

GETTING STARTED WITH COMPUSERVE

Taking on what I considered the all-powerful CompuServe was a big step for me. I'd first heard of CompuServe back in 1983 when I got my first computer with a built-in modem. But I had no reason to log on, nor did I think I could afford it. Well, you do get what you pay for, and I have since seen why CompuServe continues to be a very big voice in online communications—cost factors aside. By the way, most of the rap against

CompuServe as expensive is unfair when you consider the extensive benefits for the user.)

CompuServe is easy to log on to. The company will send you instructions and software, including their own front end, offline reader—CompuServe Information Manager (CIM) for DOS, WinCIM for Windows, and MacCIM for Mac users. (See Figure 5-8 for an example of the Information Manager for DOS.) You can also access CompuServe in ASCII (all text) from any terminal communications program. CompuServe also has (as do all the services) 800 numbers for member assistance. CompuServe may have a reputation for being "techie" and expensive, but they do a first-class job of getting you online and helping you as you go.

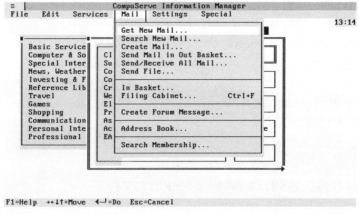

Figure 5-8. *CompuServe Information Manager for DOS*

Email

CompuServe email is easy to access through one of the offline readers or front ends for the system. You can access your emailbox "running raw" in ASCII, but there is no need to because of the CompuServe Information Manager (CIM). All my email, downloading from forums, even the bulk of my Internet emailing is done using CIM. Once you learn the program, it's easy to do.

Navigating the Hot Spots

As I do with all the other services, I recommend getting to know someone through the common interests forums in CompuServe. There are a lot of good ones, so I asked around; I've been told that the Multi-Player Games Forum has spawned a few marriages. Other popular places to meet people include the Chess, Collectibles, Gamers, and Pets/Animals forums. CompuServe has been around for over a decade and provides the user some well-structured forums that have been around a long time. One interesting example is the HSX (human sexuality) Adults and the HSX Open forums. These forums have been operating since 1984 and have served as a haven for people who needed a safe place to discuss privately everything from personal health issues, to support for survivors of abuse, to all types of non-traditional sexual lifestyles. You can also find a singles club as well as places to discuss everything from financial problems to romantic break-ups to shyness, just to name a few.

When I first logged on to CompuServe, I posted a note in the Collectibles Forum. I was lucky, because the first note I got back was from a very knowledgeable fellow, Dave Cunningham, who runs that forum on CompuServe. Dave actually owns a collectibles store and originally proposed such a forum to CompuServe, including a long description of how he envisioned the forum. About a year later, it had managed to clear all the hurdles and Dave was invited to run the Collectibles Forum. He told me that he knew enough to avoid growing too fast.

"The concept of a forum, as I see it, is close to that of a family, with siblings arriving into the family over time, rather than all at once. The Collectibles Forum, in particular, is run as an electronics club. Its members determine its shape and the direction it will go. When we started, we were primarily aimed at traditional coin and stamp collectors, and I was "chief cook and bottlewasher." As we added sections, such as Sports Cards, Autographs and Books, Dolls and Figurines, we added "section leaders" to our family, with each of them responsible for a specific subject."

Where the People Are

Of course, I wanted to know about the chat areas. Dave explained that CompuServe offers several methods of interactive chatting. The most popular one is known as "CB Simulator," in which you have thirty-six "channels" on each band (currently three separate bands, one general, one adult, and one mainly for games). In CB, you can be in one channel and monitor up to two others, at the same time that you engage in private chats with others on the system. Each channel has particular groups residing in them, so you know a bit about anyone you engage in a chat.

In the forums, the area similar to the CB Simulator is referred to as the Conference area. Many forums hold formal conferences on a regular schedule, but the rooms are always open for private chats. Frequently people who see each other regularly at conferences get to know a great deal about each other, and this may lead to in-person meetings.

There are several good offline readers and front-ends for CompuServe, including CompuServe Information Manager (CIM), offered by CompuServe to its members, as mentioned earlier. With CIM, you can easily get into a private conversation with anyone else in the forum, and you can also use the forum conference rooms for conversation. However, you can most easily have an intimate chat by using the private conversation boxes provided in the CIM software. Some of the other offline readers like Tapcis and Ozcis are not as graphical as CIM, but they are faster and use less time online. Some people use the faster offline readers for going in and out of public messaging areas and collecting postings and use CIM's convenient conferencing and private chatting features.

The Love/Sex/Friendship Connection on CompuServe

CompuServe has it all—lots of great chat areas, in all sorts of formats (ASCII with commands, or the graphical user interface with point and click options). You can use an alias in the "CB" area or just lurk around in the live conversation areas and discover who seems interesting to you. There is a very large base of different kinds of people to choose from (perhaps the most diverse of any service). There is no limit geographically, as CompuServe has the most significant global presence of any of the commercial services. Many couples have courted across the oceans (even more, of course, here in the United States). While most of this book focuses on finding new friends and lovers, cyberspace can be a huge help in holding together the IRL bonds of love and friendship over long distances and long separations.

I did the unimaginable and bought a modem for my IBM-compatible 8086—a donation from my patient, computer-literate fiancé. After adjusting the baud rate, I was online. I could now communicate with my fiancé in Raleigh, N.C., every day for less than the phone bill, which was beginning to take on a life of its own. We took full advantage of our email system. I became as addicted to my

computer as I had been addicted to CNN during the Gulf War. Reading his messages were now a part of my daily routine. I began to explore the directory for others whom I had lost touch with since moving to Washington, D.C. I was discouraged. None of my friends had entered the computer era. Could I have become a computer nerd? Before the thought had time to gel, I found someone who'd left Raleigh during my senior year and ventured out west. We kept in touch through the U.S. postal service, but I had not heard from her in a good six months. We caught up with each others' lives online.
–Kelly, a member of CompuServe,
who married her fiancé in November 1994

The Cost of CompuServe

The CompuServe Standard Pricing Plan basic services are available at unlimited connect time for under $10.00 a month. Beyond the basic services, the current hourly connect rates (subject to change) are as follows:

300 baud $4.80/hour
1200, 2400 baud $4.80/hour
9600, 14400 baud . . .$9.60/hour

You will be charged a Membership Support Fee of $2.50/month with the CompuServe Alternative Pricing Plan. This fee is charged to cover various Member Support Services. These services are provided free of connect time charges. The current hourly connect charges for the Alternative Pricing Plan are as follows:

300 baud. $6.30/hour
1200, 2400 baud $12.80/hour
9600, 14400 baud . . . $22.80/hour

The CB Club has special rates—for a monthly fee of $25, you can chat all you want, 24 hours a day, for $3 an hour. For a monthly fee of $50, you can chat all you want, 24 hours a day, for $1 an hour.

Feel and Flavor and Who Is Online

Many computer companies have their support forums on CompuServe, and a great number of clubs meet regularly online too. CompuServe has a good mix of every kind of person, in part because of its enormous size. It's like being in the largest, most organized, and efficient city you could imagine.

CompuServe has a sizable base of international users as I've mentioned before—I 've been in conferences with people from Germany. (Picking a time for a world-wide conference was a bit tricky, but we chose 11 a.m. EST on a Saturday.) Combine CompuServe's overseas membership base with CompuServe's Internet email access, and you truly have worldwide connections to everyone from the most computer-literate to experts in crafting to folks addicted to hot chatting, or to those who just enjoy using CompuServe's extensive email, news, sports, and weather features.

GETTING STARTED WITH AMERICA ONLINE

Last but not least, I logged onto America Online (AOL). AOL sent me a starter kit with access software, so all I had to do was load the software and I was online. It is very easy to log on and AOL has an attractive graphical user interface. There is software available for both Macs and Windows/DOS. As with Prodigy, you must use the AOL software anytime you go online.

Who Is Using AOL?

AOL has primarily a consumer-based audience and is a very people-oriented service. AOL appears to have a large percentage of Macintosh computer users online, probably because of AOL's roots as a Macintosh service. (DOS and Windows users can also access AOL but it catered, at one time, only to Macintosh users.). Because a lot of children use Apple computers, kids are online on AOL in big numbers. Anyone can send an instant message to anyone else online at any time. As a result, AOL has designed their service to include Parental Control, which means that the main account holder, who must be at least 18 years or older, can block instant messages sent to sub-accounts. The main account holder can also block the entry of sub-accounts into **People Connection**, the area where a lot of live chat, hot tubs, and erotic rambling goes on.

Email and More

AOL, of course, has email, but it also has email for the Internet. While on AOL you can access email groups and other information-rich areas of the Internet. Thanks to AOL's access software with its offline reader capabilities built in, everything you find online or in your email box can be saved to a file that you can read and work with when you are offline.

Navigating on AOL

Navigation is fairly simple with AOL; the graphic interface allows you to point and click using the icons and menus at the top of the screen. (You can also use keywords to go directly to where you want to go.) Those icons at the top of your screen are a quick way to access some of the more popular spots online with AOL. Like all the national services, AOL has an extensive help area, too, at no charge. AOL doesn't look like Prodigy, but it is easy to use in much the same way Prodigy is. Each screen has something of interest and entices you to click on its icon—and you're there.

Finding People

It is very easy to find out if someone is online with AOL. Just click on "Members" on the menu bar on the top of the screen, and from there you can get information on locating a member, see if they are online, send an instant message, or edit your online profile, and it's all very easy to do. (See Figure 5-9 for an example of AOL's Welcome screen.)

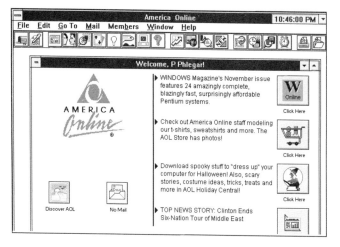

Figure 5-9. *America Online's welcome screen*

As soon as you log on, you can also choose the People Connection icon on the top of your screen—the icon is the image of one person whispering in another's ear. There are other icons across the top of your screen that can bring you close to those online (for example, Lifestyles and Interests). This area's icon is a postage stamp and a magnifying glass, representing hobbies like stamp collecting and other recreational entertainment.

Dating/Mating/Fooling Around Game

AOL was the first service to provide a easy way for anyone online to talk to anyone else online. When I've called AOL for help and information, I've found them to be very serious about serving their customers. I also got some very interesting information too: On AOL, over fifteen hundred chat rooms can be open at one time, and there are chat rooms in most of the forums throughout AOL. For all the hot chatting going on in the popular People Connection, the woman I spoke to on the phone most recently was preaching to the choir when she said "the best places to meet people are in the forums, and the best way to meet them is not to try to meet anyone, just have fun." When chatting live or reading someone's public posts, you can use the bio options, too, so you have some idea (assuming the person is being somewhat honest!) of what that person is all about, provided they've entered a bio.

And then there is the Romance Connection, just the spot for singles looking for a mate. Romance Connection is a cyberspace dating service; there's a place for you to discuss your preferences, from geographical to sexual.

There is a wide variety of cybersex on AOL: one-on-one meetings are prevalent, but AOL's "Hot Tubs" are infamous for the group sexual activity (fantasized, of course) that goes on those rooms. But if this type of sexual activity is not for you, AOL's public bulletin board areas are crammed with interesting people with something besides sex on their minds.

While going through a divorce, I tried cybersex but found that even online, casual, meaningless, emotionless sex was not really my style. I did it for awhile but found that it wasn't what I needed. What I needed was someone to know, to be close to, to please. Someone who could make me feel desired. I needed to know that I was still desirable. (Divorces tend to shake your confidence!)

Even in cyberspace, one doesn't make love all the time. One has to talk on occasion. I found that I was asking about my cyberlovers' lives. Trying to find out more about them. And I revealed more about myself as well. As I found out more, I became closer to these women. They were no longer anonymous, but had problems and involvements, but also victories to celebrate.

Once I began learning more, the relationships I had with them became more real. It became more difficult to juggle a number of women at the same time. There were people I actually wanted to be with; who wanted to be with me; and it became increasingly difficult to take enough time to be with all of them.

Eventually, I met a woman online who was unlike the others. Kay was open and honest in a way that few ever had been. She had a different way of looking at things. She challenged me because her thought processes were different, and sometimes difficult to keep up with. Kay couldn't be figured out easily. She constantly kept me on my toes. We made love online, but not right at first, she'd never done it, had little interest in it, and said no. After a few months of chatting as friends, she agreed to try cybersex, and for me, it was different. It felt more real, somehow. We had more in common than I had with most of the other women I'd been with online. We had more to talk about. We became friends.

We argued at times; we made up. And gradually, I lost my interest in the casual "affairs" I'd had online, and spent most of my available time talking with my friend. Sometimes making love,

sometimes not. We've planned to meet, Kay and I. I wonder how it will turn out. I wonder whether I can feel about her in person the way I do online. Who knows what might happen?"
—Stephen, on America Online

Cost of Service

AOL is $9.95 a month, which allows for five online hours. Each additional hour is $3.50. If you like to chat, your time on AOL can add up. I'd suggest keeping track of your time online—maybe pick a particular length of time that you'll use for chatting and set your watch or your computer's alarm clock. Though AOL may seem expensive, you get what you pay for in terms of ease of use and available services.

Feel and Flavor

AOL is bright and colorful and, as I've mentioned, very easy to use. While in People Connection, you'll feel like you've stumbled into a shopping center of parties! There are rooms for everyone with every type of interest, and if you can't find yours, you can create your own. Within minutes you'll have a great group of folks dropping by to chat. Sometimes the talk seems meaningless and sometimes it will be a bit more serious. Most of the actual cybersex goes on in private rooms. Suddenly you're speaking to someone through an instant message, and a chat—perhaps a friendship—begins.

AND DON'T FORGET...

There are some basics you should keep in mind before actually joining any service:

- A credit card is very helpful for ease of use, though some services will do automatic transfers from your checking account.

- Ask friends of yours who are already online to give you a tour of the service they use, and ask them what they like about it.
- If you decide you don't like the service you've tried, do some research. Most of them have a trial period, either in the form of a few free hours or a money back guarantee.

Once you are online, keep the following in mind:

- Be prepared to feel overwhelmed, but remember that this feeling will go away with time.
- Try to take advantage of everything the service has to offer. There may be options and opportunities you haven't uncovered that will interest you.
- After you've taken time to investigate these services, you'll begin to get your own feel for those you like and which ones will work for you.
- Take your time learning what there is available in any given service—each has a lot to offer.
- The national services are extremely safe and secure, but you can get yourself in trouble if you divulge too much personal information. On the other hand, the Internet is less secure, and you should keep that in mind when you use it.
- It's going to take time to meet people who interest you, and the common-interest bulletin boards and forums are the best place to meet people you'll like and who will like you—just be patient, don't try too hard, and enjoy yourself.
- Expect your writing skills to be tested; many people find that being online forces them to become better writers and communicators.

SUMMARY OF SERVICES

There are so many options to choose from when going online that it's worth a quick review. For the most inexpensive chatting, there's Delphi. For graphics and ease of use, try AOL—which will be relatively expensive if you're online for hours a night. Consider this: 20 hours a month (including time spent sending all the email you care to write) on Delphi is $20, but 20 hours a month (including the email time) on AOL is $9.95 for the first 5 hours, and an additional $3.50 for the other 15 hours—bringing your monthly AOL bill to $62.45. I don't think that $62.45 is unreasonable when you consider what AOL has to offer. But if you don't like or care about graphical interfaces and prefer navigating in text mode, Delphi is wonderfully inexpensive and you are still getting the same basic service: communication. If live chatting is not a priority, GEnie and CompuServe may be what you're looking for. Both of them have extensive public messaging areas which, through offline readers, can be accessed very cheaply. You'd stay very busy, if for example, if you managed to use up GEnie's four hours each month just on public messaging and emails!

Prodigy may seem expensive at first glance, but has a lot to offer in its Value Plan—a lot of features are available in the Core for which you have an unlimited amount of time, day or night. On the other hand, with the different choices like the CB club special pricing and faster baud rates for downloading on CompuServe (which also has a "use anytime" basic service area), you could discover ways to use that service most efficiently, too. CompuServe provides a higher cost to access the service at a faster modem speed (9600 baud) in some areas—perfect for downloading messages and files because the speed more than makes up for the higher price. But for chatting, the lower baud rates work just as well as and more cheaply than the fast ones.

If you use a calculator and a little planning, you'll find that all the services have something affordable and interesting for you. I think the national services are great places to meet a large, diverse group of people for a very reasonable price; for the most part, they have addressed the need of their members to meet others through the live chat areas, interesting forums, and personal ads. The bottom line is that you have to decide. For professional reasons, I subscribe to all the services and love being able to choose whatever online world I'm in the mood for. But that is not possible for everyone.

All the national online services have voice numbers for assistance, along with documentation to help you learn about the service of your choice. See the Appendix for more information on getting technical help and, in some cases, software for the national services.

CHAPTER SIX
▶
The Internet

The Internet is a global "network of networks" connecting more than three million separate computers and at least twenty million individuals. The Internet began as a U.S. government-funded network for the exchange of data between military organizations and the institutions and universities doing work for the government; now, major Internet growth is occurring in the commercial and private sectors. The computers running each of the commercial services and each local BBS are contained in a specific site; the services they offer are easy to define, and they each have a distinct personality and appearance. The Internet, by contrast, seems sprawling and multifaceted. It's in many ways the sum of its parts, and no one person or entity controls it.

In this chapter you'll get a glimpse of the width and breadth of the person-to-person connections available on the Internet. Socializing on the Internet is different from the commercial services and BBSs primarily only in that your opportunities for meeting people are so greatly increased and the kinds of experiences you can have vary widely. While the services offer specific places for you to go to hook up with friends and strangers, on the Internet you have to know where you're going, how to get there, and what activities occur in a particular place.

GETTING TO THE INTERNET

There are several ways to get access to the Internet. While businesses and institutions may choose to get a full connection to the Internet (through leased phone lines), this is a pretty expensive way to go. Home users can go through a **service provider**, a company in business solely to sell Internet access to individuals who want it by offering direct or dialup connections to the Internet. A **dialup connection** means you simply call into a modem-equipped computer that actually has the connection to the Internet; while you're there, you have access to its Internet features and hard disk space. It looks like you're doing things from your own computer, but all the transactions are really going on in the computer that you're logged on to. The **direct connection** is a more powerful way of connecting to the Internet at greater bandwidth; you make the actual link with the Internet through the SLIP/PPP protocol. If you want to know more about all this, consult some of the other books listed in the Appendix. The nice thing about going through a service provider is that you don't have to learn the details of making the connection—the service provider handles it for you.

Costs

You can sign up for a variety of Internet access packages at widely varying prices. Some services charge a monthly fee for an allotted amount of time, others charge on an hour-by-hour basis. Charges on the Internet can vary greatly. For example, it's about $2.75 an hour, for a $10 a month minimum, for access any time of the day on some local carriers. On Delphi (a national service), using the Internet with Delphi's $3 monthly charge and a connection between 6 p.m. and 7 a.m. weekdays and all hours on weekends, it's as little as $1 an hour if you're on Delphi's 20 hours for $20 program. The relatively new and still growing national service BBS Direct/CRIS packs a big value as it provides unlimited Internet access, access to the BBSs they carry from all over the country, and access to the CRIS information service for $30 a month. (You can get more information on BBS Direct/CRIS in the Appendix; prices are subject to change.) Other carriers also provide low rates for off-hours with a small basic fee; you need to shop around for a package that suits your schedule and budget.

Getting Around

Once you get an Internet account, you'll still have to get up to speed on navigating the Internet. While there are some graphical user interfaces that make cruising the Internet much easier, a lot of it is still text-based, and navigating is done through UNIX commands. If you're using communications software that is text-based, you have to know the various commands used to go somewhere, download files, or send messages. Refer to the Internet resources in the Appendix. They can help you along your way.

INTERNET ACCESS THROUGH THE COMMERCIAL SERVICES

If you're already on a national online service or a BBS with an Internet link, go to the Internet forum. There you'll find lots of useful information on how to access the Internet and the Internet services provided. All have email, some have newsgroups and mailing lists, some have information search capabilities, a few have live chat capabilities, and some provide full access. (With the proper equipment, you can also download audio and video clips where they are available, but plan on upgrading your hard drive.)

SENDING MAIL

One of the easiest things to do on the Internet is send and receive email. Of course, you need someone to send it to. You might already know someone who has an Internet address or is on another national service. For most national services, the Internet address will be the user's (ID)@(name of the service).com. You no longer have to be on the same online service to stay in touch with friends online because all of the national services and many BBSs have at least an Internet email gateway. Thus, if you're on a national online service, you already have an Internet address. For example, if your ID on AOL was Sweetie, your sample address would be sweetie@aol.com. Similarly, if your ID on Delphi was Sweetie, your sample address would be sweetie@delphi.com. With GEnie, it's a little different and would be sweetie@geis.genie.com. (On CompuServe the comma on your numerical ID would be a period instead.) You can now be in touch with millions of people all around the world almost instantaneously, and a global missive costs no more than a message sent across town.

Here is an Internet message I received from my editor at *Boardwatch Magazine*:

```
Subject:+Postage Due+PLAYING WITH BARBIE
Date: 20-Jun-94 at 13:22
From: INTERNET:brian.gallagher@boardwatch.com
To:  Phyllis Phlegar,71562,407
Sender: brian.gallagher@boardwatch.com
Received: from netcomsv.netcom.com by dub-img-2.compuserve.com
    (8.6.4/5.940406sam) id
PAA28897; Mon, 20 Jun 1994 15:21:04 -0400
From: <brian.gallagher@boardwatch.com>
Received: from boardwatch.com by netcomsv.netcom.com with UUCP
    (8.6.4/SMI-4.1)id
MAA22329; Mon, 20 Jun 1994 12:20:00 -0700
Received: by boardwatch.com
id OESZTO4E Mon, 20 Jun 94 10:32:20 MST
Message-Id: <9406201032.0ESZT04@boardwatch.com>
Organization: Boardwatch Magazine
X-Mailer: TBBS/PIMP v3.09
Date: Mon, 20 Jun 94 10:32:20 MST
```

Subject: PLAYING WITH BARBIE
To: 71562.407@compuserve.com
Dear Phyllis,
Thanks for getting this to me, I'll let you know as soon as I can. Brian

Notice how many lines of routing information you get before receiving the actual message. That gives you an idea of how large and complex a system of smaller networks the Internet really is. For other Internet communication shown in this chapter, I'll leave off all the header information.

Here's something that you need to keep in mind: The language of the Internet is what is known as UNIX, which is case–sensitive. If a command is "W50" it's not the same as "w50." Internet addresses must be all in lower case. You'll notice that beside "SENDER" is Brian's address, and it is all in lower case. Also, you'll note that at the top of the letter it says "INTERNET:" and Brian's address too. That INTERNET: is CompuServe's command, or way of routing a message to the Internet, and not somewhere within the CompuServe member list. Each of the national services has its own protocol for sending messages to the Internet.

ONLINE THROUGH THE OFFICE

Many people get their Internet access through their employer, but I urge you not to conduct personal relations through your company's online connections. Why not? Because it compromises your privacy; other people in the company can access your email or anything you receive on the Internet. I heard a horror story about Internet email. When an employee was laid off, apparently due to internal politics involving the MIS (Management Information Systems) manager, the MIS manager was able to read all of his private mail (she claimed thought the messages were posted publicly and blamed him for her not knowing the difference) and used it against him in memos she circulated around the office. Luckily, he was not carrying on any intimate exchanges on the Internet, only business-related ones. Even so, his offhand remarks about the company that employed him and the responses he received privately were presented publicly as reasons why he could not be trusted. The MIS manager's attitude was that the company owned the address, and she thought she had a right to read items addressed to him. Fair or not, the bottom line was she was able to access his supposedly private email and ruin his credibility, and he had no way to defend himself once he left the company.

You may say that a work environment is no place to be making personal contacts. That's true, but people meet in the office, on the phone, and *online*, and sometimes become personally involved. If and when you meet someone online through your office email address and want to take the relationship further, get your own Internet address. And if you think that a company *does* have the right to break into personal email written while at work, do they also have the right to tape, and listen to personal phone conversations while at work, to watch you in the lavatory or open personal U.S. mail that you sent from work? Since the company also owns the computers, the phones, the lavatories, and the baskets to put U.S. mail in, and since some of this activity might be occurring during a break or off-hours (lunch, and so on), acceptable use of company resources is sometimes not a clearly defined area. These issues are the stuff of lawsuits, and you should be aware of them when deciding when and where to conduct personal email business.

ETIQUETTE

The Internet, while constantly growing and changing in many ways, has its own traditions of etiquette and discourse. The Internet's main reason for being is as a conduit for the free flow of information. You'll find some perfectly tame, even boring discussions going on at points within the Internet, and you can also stumble onto some very explicit discussions on matters of sex, cybersex, and alternate lifestyles. If what you happen to find offends you or isn't quite your style, leave. There are plenty of other places to go.

Keep a few basic rules in mind as you wander and engage in your Internet pursuits:

- **Be considerate, tolerant, and respectful of others, their opinions, and their prose**. This applies equally in other online areas, but it's worth repeating here.
- **Chill out before flaming**. Take time before responding in anger or irritation. Once you send a message out, it's gone and can't be taken back.
- **Read before you write**. Take the time to get a feel for the kind of interaction that goes on in a certain place before jumping in. This might take a few minutes, or you may feel more comfortable visiting a few days before formally getting in on the action.
- **Keep confidential information to yourself**. Again, this seems like a given for any reasonable person, but with the ease of online communication, something you tell someone else can be broadcast over the world in a matter of seconds. Check with your source before repeating something you think may be personal or private information.

WHERE CAN YOU MEET PEOPLE?

While you can certainly get a lot out of private email with people, there are several kinds of group forums for socializing and exchanging information on the Internet: mailing lists, Usenet newsgroups, Internet Relay Chat (IRC), and Multi-User Dungeons (MUDs). As with the BBSs and commercial services, I'd advise picking out a service on a topic that interests you and joining in.

Mailing Lists

There are thousands of mailing lists on the Internet. These lists exist for people with similar interests to exchange email among themselves. If, for example, you were on a single-parents board either locally or nationally, you might also want to join a mailing list of single parents on the Internet. You subscribe to a list by sending email to a list's administrative address, which is the email address of the person who owns the list. Once you're added to the list, you'll begin to receive email deliveries of messages on your topic. These deliveries can be daily for some of the more active lists or weekly for a list that sees less traffic.

As a subscriber, you have the option of only reading the messages, replying to the messages that interest you, or even suggesting new topics for discussion.(These must relate to the main theme of the list.) You can send messages to all members of a list, a subset of the list, or send private replies to a list member.

Most lists are open to anyone who wishes to join, but some require the approval of either the list owner or moderator. Subscriber address information can be made public to people outside the list on public lists; in private lists, only subscribers know who is participating in their lists. In order to cut down on the junk mail generated in mailing lists and to keep the quality of the discussion of a certain level, some lists are moderated. Most lists, however, aren't.

Here are some examples of the issues covered in mailing lists:

Network-wide ID	TOPIC@NODE	List title
MCUG–L'	MCUG–L@MIAMIU	Alternative Colorful Postings
ADND–L	ADND–L@PUCC	Advanced Dungeons and Dragons
AIDS	AIDS@EBOUB011	AIDS Newsgroup
ASTROL–L	ASTROL–L@BRUFPB	Astrological Discussion
AUTORACE	AUTORACE@INDYCMS	Discussion of Auto Racing
BEE–L	BEE–L@ALBNYVM1	Discussion of Bee Biology
BIFEM–D	BIFEM–D@BROWNVM	Bisexual Women's Discussion List
BIRD_RBA	BIRD_RBA@ARIZVM1	National Birding Hotline Cooperative
BISEXU–D	BISEXU–D@BROWNVM	Bisexual Digest
BISEXU–L	BISEXU–L@BROWNVM	Bisexuality Discussion List
BUDDHA–L	BUDDHA–L@ULKYVM	Buddhism Discussion Group
CANINE–L	CANINE–L@PCCVM	Discussion Forum for Dog Fanciers
CHRISTIA	CHRISTIA@ASUACAD	Practical Christian Life
DRUGABUS	DRUGABUS@UMAB	Drug Abuse Education Information
FEMSEM	FEMSEM@SBCCVM	Stony Brook Feminist Philosophy
FNORD–L	FNORD–L@UBVM	New Ways of Thinking List
GRANOLA	GRANOLA@BROWNVM	Vegetarian Discussion List
GRUNGE–L	GRUNGE–L@UBVM	Grunge Rock Discussion List
HEBREW–L	HEBREW–L@UMINN1	Jewish & Near Eastern Studies
ISLAM–L	ISLAM–L@ULKYVM	History of Islam
LAIDOFF	LAIDOFF@ARIZVM1	So, You've Been Laid Off?
MAC–L	MAC–L@YALEVM	Macintosh News and Information
MSLIST–L	MSLIST–L@NCSUVM	Multiple Sclerosis
RAILROAD	RAILROAD@PCCVM	The Railroad List

RECYCLE	RECYCLE@UMAB	Recycling in Practice
SCUBA-L	SCUBA-L@BROWNVM	Scuba Diving Discussion List
SKATING	SKATING@UMAB	Figure Skating Fans
STAMPS	STAMPS@PCCVM	The Stamps List
STARGAME	STARGAME@PCCVM	Star Trek Role Playing Game List
STOPRAPE	STOPRAPE@BROWNVM	Sexual Assault Activist List
STORM-L	STORM-L@UIUCVMD	Storms and Weather Related Info
THEATRE	THEATRE@GREARN	The Theatre Discussion List
WRITERS	WRITERS@NDSUVM1	Writers Discussion List

People Connecting In Newsgroups

Another forum on the Internet that puts you in contact with people who share your interests is Usenet newsgroups. Newsgroups are discussions on a specific topic, and you'll often find related articles and files of interest there. Newsgroups are similar to email lists except that messages posted to newsgroups are sent to the computer that carries Usenet; with mailing lists, every message you post gets sent directly to each subscriber's emailbox.

Each participating Usenet computer selects the newsgroups it carries; there are thousands of newsgroups, and not all newsgroups will be available on each site. Your Internet service provider, some of the national services, and many BBSs will have a list of newsgroups for you to choose from, and you can subscribe to the ones that interest you.

If you're getting your Internet access through a commercial online service, you won't need special software to access newsgroups (it's built into the interface you use for your service, or is otherwise made available through the service). But if you have a separate Internet access through a service provider that does not have a newsreader, you will need it to read or post news to newsgroups. However, most Internet providers have newsreaders.

Newsgroups are organized according to category, and you can identify what category a newsgroup belongs to by its prefix.

Here is a list of the major categories:

Category	Description
comp	related to computers
rec	recreational activities and hobbies
sci	related to the sciences
soc	groups discussing social issues or groups that exist for socializing
misc	miscellaneous; groups that don't belong to the other established categories
talk	groups that debate current events or issues
news	related to Usenet

There are also minor or alternative categories of newsgroups. The main category, identified by the alt prefix, indicates a discussion group that is informal, controversial, or "alternative" in nature. Some of the alt newsgroups see the heaviest traffic; you can find interesting and sometimes fairly bizarre conversations going on in alt newsgroups. Other categories include biz (business-related newsgroups), bionet (biology-related newsgroups), k12 (education-related newsgroups), and others.

Here's a sample of available newsgroups:

alt.personals
alt.personals.ads
alt.sex.voyeurism
alt.personals
alt.abuse–recovery
alt.amazon–women.admirers
alt.american.olympians.choke.choke.choke
alt.alien.visitors

alt.art.theft.scream.scream.scream
alt.astrology
alt.fan.tonya–harding.whack.whack.whack
misc.jobs.offered
rec.collecting
rec.crafts.quilting
rec.food.recipes
rec.games.bridge
rec.humor
rec.pets
sci.physics.edward.teller.boom.boom.boom

Once you get your Usenet access, look for the news.announce.new users newsgroup, which contains a history of Usenet and a list of the various newsgroups available. Your newsreader allows you to select the newsgroups you want to participate in. As with mailing lists, you subscribe to a newsgroup itself—not to the address of an actual person. After joining a newsgroup, you should take time to read the **Frequently Asked Questions** (FAQ) file . This contains important information on the newsgroup; it usually includes a description of what the newsgroup exists for and a list of FAQs about the newsgroup. The following is taken from the FAQ from one of the more colorful newsgroups on the Internet:

> **Subj:** FAQ alt.society.underwear
> **Question:** So why is this here?
>
> alt.society.underwear was established as a forum to discuss society's views of underwear—what it implies, what it means, how people react to it, and how YOU as a person react to these reactions. People have widely different views about how underwear relates to their sexual and daily lives.
>
> Some people consider it merely the clothing under their clothing,

others consider it an essential component of sexuality (witness the popularity of lingerie boutiques and similar establishments). In any case, society, in general, discourages attribution of desire or anything else to underwear—leaving alt.society.underwear with a mission.

Question: What do I post?

Anything you want—scanned pictures, stories, discussion threads from other groups—that has to do with underwear.

Question: Why are most of the references in this FAQ related to women's underwear?

Because I'm a man and, well, I really don't care personally much for men's underwear. But, as this group gets traffic, there will doubtlessly be discussions about those as well. As these discussions come into being, they will be included in this FAQ as the group develops.

REAL-TIME TALKING

There's no live interaction with other people through mailing lists and newsgroups. Messages and articles are created, posted, stored, and then eventually make their way to the intended recipients. You read postings made hours or days ago, and your responses are read by others sometime later. If you're looking for instant communication with people on the Internet, there are several live chat options. We'll take a look at Internet Relay Chat (IRC) and Multi-User Dungeons (MUDs) next.

Internet Relay Chat (IRC)

Real-time chat on the Internet is known as Internet Relay Chat or IRC. Through the IRC service, you can either chat on more than a thousand existing channels or pick a topic and form a channel of your own. If you are interested in this type of global interaction, make sure you subscribe to an Internet Service

Provider with IRC capabilities. IRC is like the CB radio of the Internet. Talking on an IRC channel is not unlike a conference call or a big dinner with everyone sitting at the same table; some folks are talking to everyone, and others are just listening.

Once a channel is created, its place in the system is held by a robot, or "bot." I stumbled into a channel called #computer sex, which listed only one person being present. I thought it would be interesting to see what one person was doing in the room or channel devoted to computer sex, but after joining the channel I discovered this person was actually the robot. This seemed pretty funny to me at the time—the computer version of the blowup sex doll!

The following is an excerpt from a conversation that went on in a channel called #Internet, appropriately enough. You'll notice that people join and leave as the conversation goes on—there always seem to be new people popping in out of nowhere. Two of the participants were from outside the U.S., and I admired their bravery to converse in a second language in the already challenging, word-dependent world of cyberspace. I've left their responses just as they gave them, sometimes in broken English.

>   *** Yarasin (~HH@d1_pc12.PClabs.metu.edu.tr) has joined channel #internet
>   <Jim> Hi Yarasin.
>   <Yarasin> hi everybody.
>   <Phyllis> How do you guys like the IRC?
>   <weef> say I don't know how to use IRC.
>   <Phyllis >Weef, you are using IRC right now!
>   <weef> say I know..but I am kinda confused...
>   <Yarasin> yes you are
>   <Yarasin> r u fr japanese
>   <weef> say well is this part right...i mean..am i supposed to use

"say?!"
<weef> say well, I came here cause there were people..can you recommend a channel where I can kinda figure this out?
<Jim> Weef: you can join the channel #irchelp to get the best irc help.
<weef> say thanks jim....now all I have to to is get out
*** Signoff: weef (Leaving)
<Burner> phyllis do you work for some type of publication?
<Phyllis> Yes, I do.
<Burner> Thought so. A mag or news?
<Yarasin> i am turkey
<Phyllis> You're in Turkey?!
<Yarasin> yes
<Phyllis> Burner, why did you ask if I work for some type of publication?
<Jim> Because you are curious.
<Yarasin> it possible
*** JanB (~JB@dsr.us.net) has joined channel #internet
<Phyllis> Since I do, it was an unusual coincendence!
<Yarasin> r u studi
<Burner> So this is lunch break IRC...!!!.
<Yarasin> wht r u doing your in life
<JanB> I am a Dutch intern in the US and am keeping in touch with my friends this wayy... except they are all gone now...getting a little late in europe
<Phyllis> Jan, you are in the Netherlands?
<Yarasin> hw can help youte, too
<JanB> Nope I am Maryland now... But usually I am in the Netherlands
<JanB> Hoping to meet some interesting people from abroad ??
<Yarasin> it possible

<Phyllis> I see...are you originally from the USA or Netherlands?
<JanB> I am from the Netherlands...I usually go on the internet from there.
<Phyllis> Oh, I see Jan!
<Phyllis> Jan, I bet you really like using the Internet to keep in touch!
<JanB> Yep...At my Faculty in the Netherlands everyone has an Internet Address
*** Burner has left channel #internet
<JanB> So are you going to be on the Internet more or is this a one time outing..... .
<Phyllis> I will probably be on more.
<JanB> gotta go and get back to my "job".

Beyond IRC

If you're looking to meet others live on the Internet, there are many interpersonal, extra-textual adventures you can seek out. A MUD (Multi-User Dungeon) is a multiplayer role-playing game based on particular themes and scenarios. There are many other variants of the MUD, including MUSHs (Multi-User Shared Hallucination), MOOs (MUD Object-Oriented), TinyMUDS, and more. MUDers and MUSHers interact in a virtual environment that simulates an entirely made up world, or someplace existing in a past, present, or future world, such as a medieval castle or another galaxy. Some MUDs are gamelike (a player kills creatures, engages in battle, and so on), while other MUDs are conversation and dialogue–based, existing primarily for socializing and exchanging information. MUDs and other types of teleconferencing make up roughly 50% of the chat that exists on, or just a side road off of, the Internet's information superhighway.

One of the other types of teleconferencing is a side street off that side road, known as Coffee House. Teleconferencing in this context means to **telnet** to another system. When you telnet to another system, you are, in effect, on that system directly and give commands to control that computer as you chat or do whatever. I had a flat tire on one of my early trips on the superhighway and ended up in a part of the Coffee House, quite by accident. I didn't realize that I'd skidded off the road, either. (To get to Coffee House, or wherever I was, telnet to 128.198.1.116, which is the Internet address of that particular system. It was one of the funniest cyberchatting nights I've ever had. My nickname for the adventure was "Pink" on line 40. You choose a new nickname each time you enter a channel—names are not reserved and exist only for the time that you spend on a certain channel.

Here's how part of my visit to the Coffee House went:

> (40, Pink) Just curious, how about a roll call...where is everyone from?
> (7, Fiyaka) South Carolina
> (3, comet) ;is heading towards Jupiter
> (14, Phishman) albuqueruqe new mexico
> (8) Gidget is from colorado.
> (37, Weasel) New Bedford,MA
> (38) Darkwing Duck is from wyoming...
> (48) Gent bows to all the kewl people on here.
> (40, Pink) Fiyaka, Phishman, Gidget, Weasel, Darkwing, Lana... thank you!
> (7, Fiyaka) I got to go folks, bye!!!!
> (15) Kip is from Victoria
> (8) Gidget smiles at pink
> (40, Pink) Pink smiles back at Gidget.

(48) Gent bows again to all the KEWL people on here.
(40, Pink) Anyone else care to give your state a plug?
(3, comet) lets give pink a PLUG!!!!!
(37) Weasel would love to give his state a plug. :-)
(4, Man of the 90's) TENNESSEE!!!!!!
(48, Gent) GEORGIA IS UNDER WATER!
(13) Lucifer is outta here...things to do...
>> (13) Lucifer just left.
(15, Kip) anyone wanna talk?
(2, Manly Man) ILLINOIS!!!!!!!!!!!!!
>> (2) Manly Man has wandered off.
(33, Sexual Ketchup) hi trick
>> New arrival from ingate.microsoft.com on line 8.
(3, comet) is bill gates on line 8?
>> New arrival from cns.cscns.com on line 10.
(*46, Eight Inch Probe*) hi everyone
(48) Gent wants to know where the REAL ladies are tonight? Any on here?
(40, Pink) I am being very nerdy tonight and asking where everyone is from...
(17, Prince Axtor) Nerds suck. I killed 5 of them earlier today.
(*53, beth*) men suck!!!!!
(*46, pink panther*) INVISIBLE COWS CONTROL MY DESTINY
(13, helen of troy) delaware
(40, Pink) Too obvious I guess that I am new. Thanks Helen. Anyone else?
(15) Kip is from Victoria
(33) Sexual Ketchup yawns

(33, Sexual Ketchup) so who here fantasizes about me when they sleep
(*33, Sexual Ketchup*) anyone?
(*32, da steve guy*) I fantasize about you when i eat french fries!!
>> (33) Sexual Ketchup just left.
(37,p Weasel) Hey Pink type .cPink
.cPink
>> Channel now: 'Pink'
>> (40) Pink has joined.
>> (37) Weasel has joined.
(37, Weasel) Hello
(40, Pink) How did I end up in here? Hep me hep me! Where iz i?!
(37, Weasel) Calm down.
(37, Weasel) You changed rooms with the .c command
(40, Pink) So whassup?
(37, Weasel) When you typed .cPink you created this room.
(40, Pink) What room is this, (what room was I in?!)
(37, Weasel) This room is called Pink. you were in a room called 0
(37, Weasel) Well, do you need some help with some of the commands?
(40, Pink) I am shamelessly ignorant about the Internet! I need lots of help.
(37) Weasel laughs. I can't explain the whole internet to you but I can help here.
(40, Pink) What?! Whattaya mean, you can't explain the whole Internet?! HA! ;-)

Obviously I need to do some additional brushing up on telnetting—good thing my fellow telnetters were very friendly and quite willing to help me.

As is the case everywhere you go online, the quality of the "conversation" depends on where you are and who is there with you. As you explore, you'll stumble into discussions and chats that seem neither to make much sense nor exist for any reason other than for bawdy banter or idle chatter; you'll also find well-organized, carefully moderated thoughtful discussions on a range of topics and events.

KNOW WHERE YOU WANT TO GO IN THIS WILD AND WOOLLY FRONTIER

The Internet is vast, at times unpredictable and intimidating, constantly changing, but with a little practice and perseverance, you'll get the hang of it. Wherever you go on the Internet, remember that your best tactic as a newcomer is to observe first, then ask somebody a question if you're unsure of how to participate. Occasionally you'll run into some self-righteous people who seem to resent your being new to the party, but there are always plenty of others who will make you feel at home and welcome. Generally, if you go somewhere just for chatting, you'll find there are fewer rules and conventions. People are there to make friends and to socialize. Some of the mailing lists and newsgroups have more of a sense of etiquette and acceptable behavior; it's wise to decide what you want from your experience on the Internet. Is it information and perhaps the chance to meet others who share your interests? Or is it a late-night live chat? One thing is for sure, you have plenty of options for meeting people on the Internet.

CYBERSPACE AND LOVE

The online universe is here to stay; and while it can't replace life as we knew it before online communications were available to all of us, it can add an important and enriching dimension. We can now be connected with so many people so quickly, easily, and cheaply! We can stay in touch with people who we've come to care deeply for, and with people we've moved away from.

I hope this book has given you an idea of what going online is really like and provided you with some basic tips on how to safely and enjoyably seek out new connections. The online world is not without its problems—it is, after all, only a reflection and extension of the physical world—but it contains incredible potential for meeting new people and socializing, and maybe, if you're one of the lucky ones, good friends and a lifelong love.

APPENDIX

WHAT YOU NEED TO GET CONNECTED

First, there are the hardware basics that you'll need to connect to any service:

- **A computer**. If you're using a high-speed (14,400 baud and above) modem, you should ensure that your computer has a high-speed serial port, with a 16550 chip, or get an internal modem.

- **A modem**. Since you can get a high-speed (14,400 baud and above) for less than $75, don't even consider anything slower!

- **A phone line**. The phone line will be tied up while you're online, and if you have call waiting, it could knock you offline when a call comes in. At some point your usage habits might require a dedicated line for the exclusive use of the phone line for your modem.

You'll also need software to put on top of the hardware. You'll either need communications software, or software that is specific to the service you sign on to, or both.

- **Terminal communications software**:
    ProComm (IBM compatible shareware)
    Telix (IBM compatible shareware)
    Qmodem (IBM compatible shareware)
    ProComm Plus for DOS or Windows (IBM compatible)
    Qmodem Pro for Windows (IBM compatible)
    Telix for Windows (IBM compatible)
    Microphone Pro 2.0 (Macintosh)
    Crosstalk for Macintosh
    White Knight V.12 (Macintosh)
    Zterm (Macintosh shareware)

- **Service-specific software:**
    Prodigy
    America Online (AOL)
    CompuServe Navigator
    CompuServe Information Manager
    Aladdin (for GEnie)
    eWorld (Macintosh only)

Most online services today, with the exception of CompuServe and GEnie, do not charge extra for high-speed access (in most cases, 9600 baud). This is another reason to consider at least a 14,400 baud modem when making your purchase. Another consideration is that for a little more money (approximately $20 at the time of this writing), you can also get built-in FAX capability! If you are purchasing a high-speed modem for a Macintosh, make sure you get a "hardware handshake" modem cable—this is a must for reliable high-speed communications.

Voice Contact Information for the Major Online Services

```
Prodigy ................................1-800-Prodigy
CompuServe ..........................1-800-848-8199
America Online ......................1-800-827-6364
GEnie ................................1-800-638-9636
Delphi ............................... 1-800-695-4005
BBS Direct/CRIS .....................1-800-745-2747
```

BOOKS

There are dozens of books on the Internet and the matrix of networks that make up the online world. The following list includes books and additional resources that will provide more information on the specific online route you choose.

NetGuide: Your Guide to the Services, Information and Entertainment on the Net, Michael Wolff, 1993,
Random House Inc.

The Internet Yellow Pages, Harley Hahn and Rick Stout, 1994, Osbourne/McGraw-Hill.

The E-Mail Companion, John S. Quarterman and Smoot Carl-Mitchell, 1994, Addison-Wesley Publishing Company.

The Online User's Encyclopedia: Bulletin Boards and Beyond, Bernard Aboba, 1994, Addison-Wesley Publishing Company.

The Internet Guide for New Users, Daniel P. Dern, 1993, McGraw-Hill.

The Whole Internet User's Guide and Catalogue, Second Edition, Ed Krol, O'Reilly and Associates, Inc.

The Instant Internet Guide, Brent Heslop and David Angell, 1994, Addison-Wesley Publishing Company.

The Internet Companion, Second Edition, Tracy LaQuey, 1994, Addison Wesley Publishing Company.

The Trail Guide to America Online, Jonathan Price, 1994, Addison Wesley Publishing Company.

CompuServe from A to Z: The Ultimate CompuServe Reference, Second Edition, Charles Bowen, 1994, Random House, Inc.

The Trail Guide to CompuServe, Robert R. Wiggins and Ed Tittel, 1994, Addison Wesley Publishing Company.

How to Use Prodigy, Douglas Hergert, 1994, Ziff-Davis Press.

The Trail Guide to Prodigy, Caroline M. Halliday, 1995, Addison-Wesley Publishing Company.

Glossbrenner's Master Guide to GEnie, Alfred Glossbrenner, 1991, Osbourne/McGraw-Hill.

Delphi: The Official Guide, Fourth Edition, Delphi Internet Services Corporation Staff, General VideoTex Corporation.

Modems for Dummies, Second Edition, Tina Rathbone, 1993, IDG Books.

KITS (BOOKS PLUS CONNECTION SOFTWARE)

Internet Starter Kit for the Macintosh, Adam Engst and William Dickson, 1994, Hayden Books.

The Mac Internet Tour Guide: Cruising the Internet the Easy Way, Second Edition, Michael Fraase, 1994, Ventana Press.

The Windows Internet Tour Guide: Cruising the Internet the Easy Way, Michael Fraase, 1994, Ventana Press.

The Internet Companion Plus, Second Edition, Tracey LaQuey, 1994, Addison-Wesley Publishing Company.

Internet in a Box: Complete Internet Starter Kit, Software and User Guides, 1994, O'Reilly & Associates.

MAGAZINES

Boardwatch Magazine, 800-933-6038.
This magazine lists and reviews many BBSs, and reports on the constantly changing landscape of the Internet and commercial services.

Online Access, 800-36-MODEM.
BBSs listed each month, often featured by subject. Contains articles on BBSs and the online services, and recommends places to go and things to do online.

Computer Shopper Magazine, 800-827-7889, ext. 708
This magazine has an excellent national listing for local BBSs by state and area code. This is a good place to find your first BBS so you can log on and download the list of local BBSs in your area.

Internet World, The Magazine for Internet Users 203-226-6967

GLOSSARY

Glossary

Access software Software that is provided by the service itself as the only means of signing on to that service. AOL and Prodigy provide access software.

America Online A graphically oriented commercial online service based in Vienna, Virginia. It was originally only for Mac users, but now DOS-based systems can access it.

baud rate The speed that data can be transmitted via a serial port, whether through direct connection or through a modem.

BBS Direct/CRIS Also known as the "Concentric Network" or CRC. A relatively new national online service that has, in addition to forums, chat areas, email, and full internet access, a membership of local BBSs from around the country that all users can "dial out" to, using CRC's network instead of the telephone, thus eliminating the long-distance charges.

bps Stands for bits per second. The speed at which data can travel over a data line.

bulletin board An area of common interest on a BBS or national service.

bulletin board system (BBS) A computer that users dial into to get information or use its available services.

chat mode Also known as conference mode, a feature of a BBS or national service that allows one-on-one (or more) live "real time" conferencing.

CompuServe One of the biggest commercial online services offering a staggering number of services and databases. CompuServe is based in Columbus, Ohio.

cruising Also known as surfing or skimming; checking out online areas of interest, sometimes looking for new areas.

custom forum A private area for people with fairly specialized common interests.

cybersex The term given to simulated sex through typed text transmitted over computer networks. Also known as c-sex.

cyberspace The collective online universe. Science fiction author William Gibson coined this term in his novel *Neuromancer.*

Delphi A commercial online service based in Cambridge, Massachusetts, that offers a full range of Internet services.

dialup connection A modem-based connection to the Internet.

direct connection A direct connection to an Internet node; doesn't require a modem.

download To retrieve a file of information (text, graphics, or sound) from another networked computer.

email Mail received from someone electronically.

electronic mailbox The place within your email program that your mail gets delivered to. Also referred to as emailbox.

echoes A bulletin board or forum on a network.

f2f Online abbreviation for face-to-face.

flame *n*. Unpleasant, angry, antagonistic, or inflammatory email; *v*. The act of sending such email.

flamer Someone who sends unpleasant, angry, antagonistic, or inflammatory email.

Frequently Asked Questions (FAQs) A file containing important information about a newsgroup.

front end A program that gives the service an interface whose main purpose is to enable the user to navigate more easily.

gateway The connection point between separate online systems that translates between two different protocols (or technical specifications for transmission of data).

GEnie A commercial online service based in Rockville, Maryland.

GIF   Stands for Graphical Interchange Format (originated on CompuServe). This is a file format (or technical standard) for exchanging graphical information online. Pronounced "jiff" or "giff." Some online communications systems allow users to exchange photos of themselves or other images; the specific graphic image is called a GIF.

GUI   Stands for Graphical User Interface. GUI software allows you to compute (or navigate and communicate) by a combination of pointing and clicking icons or pictures and typing in words, rather than by typing in commands only. Pronounced "gooey."

hot chat   Discussions of an erotic nature.

Internet   The interconnected network of networks, which contains thousands of separate networks and millions of individual users.

IRC   Stands for Internet Relay Chat. A global live chatting service available through the Internet.

IRL   Stands for In Real Life. Frequently seen online abbreviation used in reference to the physical world.

live chat   Stands for chatting, live! The ability to talk or type live online. Live chat allows conversation or messages to be sent and received onscreen almost instantly.

local node   A connection point that you dial into to log on to a system, be it the Internet, an online service, or BBS; a local node eliminates long distance charges.

lurking   Reading the messages in a thread or forum but not contributing any of your own; only the system operators and assistants will know you were there when they check the entry list; you will be hidden from most folks in the forum.

mailing list   Collections of email messages devoted to discussion of specific topics. You subscribe to a mailing list and receive regular deliveries of messages that the mailing list generates.

modem Stands for modulator-demodulator. The device that connects your computer to the telephone lines. When sending, it translates your digital data into analog data that can be handled by the phone lines; when receiving data, it reverses the process and turns the analog data back into digital format.

MUD Stands for Multiple User Dungeon, a simulated online environment where people engage in games or role-playing adventures or possibly just chat on a particular topic. Many MUDs simulate different environments (for instance, a space ship or a medieval castle).

newsgroups Discussion groups on the Internet available through the Usenet news feed service.

offline reader A program that gets messages and email that you've requested from the service and then presents it offline in a form that you can use both for responding to those messages and email and generating new mail and messages. Most front ends have offline readers in them.

People Connection AOL's user friendly live chat area.

postings Messages left on electronic bulletin boards.

Prodigy Prodigy is based in White Plains, New York, and is known as the most family-oriented of the services.

public message (or messaging) boards Areas where public messages are posted on a BBS. Synonymous with bulletin board or forum.

real time conference Live. The activity occurs as you read it.

Romance Connection AOL's very sophisicated "computer dating service" complete with personals arranged by preferences of geography, etc.

roundtable On the online national service GEnie, these are common interest areas with public messaging and files related to that interest; often called forums or bulletin boards on other services.

service provider A commercial Internet access provider that functions as a user's link to the Internet. Anyone with a computer and a modem can get an Internet account by purchasing access through a service provider.

SIG Stands for Special Interest Group, the common interest areas for public messaging found on Delphi. Delphi's members can open private SIGs known as **custom forums**.

signing on Making the initial connection to a specific online site.

skimming Same as **cruising**.

SLIP/PPP protocol Another type of connection to an Internet service provider. SLIP/PPP is faster than dialup and makes a transparent direct connection. This requires a front end, Mosaic being the most common. It also requires Windows and the TCP/IP network protocol. Sounds complicated but is actually relatively easy to set up.

split screen A window (usually at the bottom of the screen) provided by some software for chat. Allows you to type all your text in one window before sending it—this eliminates some of the confusion of everything that happens on the screen in a chat.

surfing Same as **cruising**.

smiley A facelike symbol (emoticon) formed using keyboard punctuation symbols. Smileys are used to express emotions or moods online, and are meant to be looked at sideways. This :) was the first smiley, but there are hundreds of commonly used variations on this theme.

sysop Stands for system operator. This is the person in charge of a BBS or a specific online forum.

s2s Online abbreviation for skin-to-skin.

telnet To connect to another computer over the Internet and in effect take control of it. Used primarily for chat and directory browsing.

terminal communications program A program that tells your modem to dial a number you've given it and to connect with an online service or BBS. It differs from access software, which is designed for only one service.

thread A grouping or collection of messages based on a certain topic; the online equivalent of a conversation or discussion between two or more individuals.

twitfiled To be twitfiled means the sysop has severely limited your access to any or all portions of a BBS, generally because of some grave social error you have committed (see **flame**).

Usenet An Internet forum of discussion groups known as **newsgroups**.

virtual Refers to the world of simulated reality that computer connections create (not real).